AFTER INDUSTRIAL SOCIETY?

THE EMERGING SELF-SERVICE ECONOMY

AFTER INDUSTRIAL SOCIETY?

The Emerging Self-service Economy

Jonathan Gershuny

Science Policy Research Unit
University of Sussex

M

© Jonathan Gershuny 1978

First published 1978 by
THE MACMILLAN PRESS LTD
London and Basingstoke
Associated companies in Delhi Dublin
Hong Kong Johannesburg Lagos Melbourne
New York Singapore and Tokyo

Printed in Great Britain by
UNWIN BROTHERS LIMITED
The Gresham Press
Old Woking, Surrey

British Library Cataloguing in Publication Data

Gershuny, Jonathan
    After industrial society.
    1. Economic history – 1945–   2. Economics
    – History – 20th century
    I. Title
    330.9′181′2   HC106.7

    ISBN 0–333–23275–5
    ISBN 0–333–23276–3   Pbk

For Esther

CONTENTS

ACKNOWLEDGEMENTS

The work on which this book is based was commissioned by the Programmes Analysis Unit, a joint unit of the U. K. Atomic Energy Authority and the Department of Industry. The opinions and arguments found here are, however, entirely those of the author, and are in no way attributable to his sponsors.

A number of people have, at various points, made helpful comments and criticisms: Peter Jones, Keith Taylor and Ken Hill from the P. A. U.; almost all of my colleagues in the Science Policy Research Unit; and in addition Christopher Saunders, Guy Routh, Krishan Kumar and Bernard Cazes. The manuscript was typed, in its various stages, by Sylvia Richards and Melanie Hempleman.

AFTER INDUSTRIAL SOCIETY – SOME SPECULATIONS

. . . the subject of history is changing and the change in approach is reflected in the words we use – new words; improvement instead of expansion, human activity instead of work, and of course one word which is quite old, liberty. (Dahrendorf, *The New Liberty*[1])

1 The Prophets' Problem

Telling the future is not always an appropriate form of behaviour. There are two separate sets of circumstances which may make it unrewarding. The first is when our predictions are wrong:

> The human race, to which so many of my readers belong, has been playing at children's games from the beginning . . . one of the games to which it is most attached is called . . . 'Cheat the Prophet'. [The prophets] took something or other that was certainly going on in their time, and then said it would go on more and more until something extraordinary happened. And very often they added that in some odd place that extraordinary thing had happened and that it shows the signs of the times. . . . The players listen very carefully and respectfully to all that the clever men have to say about what is to happen in the next generation. The players then wait until all the clever men are dead, and bury them nicely. They then go and do something else. (G. K. Chesterton, *The Napoleon of Notting Hill*[2])

Clearly, if all our forecasts are disproved, for whatever reason, there is very little point in making them. The other case is where our predictions are always right, but we cannot do anything about them:

DEATH SPEAKS: There was a merchant in Baghdad who sent his servant to market to buy provisions and in a little while the servant came back, white and trembling, and said, Master, just now when I was in the marketplace I was jostled by a woman in the crowd and when I turned I saw it was Death that jostled me. She looked at me and made a threatening gesture; now, lend me your horse, and I will go to Samarra and there Death will not find me. The merchant lent him his horse, and the servant mounted it, and he dug his spurs in its flanks and as fast as the horse could gallop he went. Then the merchant went down to the marketplace and he saw me standing in the crowd and he came to me and said, why did you make a threatening gesture to my servant when you met him this morning? That was not a threatening gesture, I said, it was only a start of surprise. I was astonished to see him in Baghdad for I had an appointment with him tonight in Samarra. (John O'Hara, *Appointment in Samarra*[3])

If we cannot avoid our nemesis we might do well not to be forewarned of it.

We are unlikely to be placed at either of these extreme positions, but the examples still point to some essential preliminary questions to any forecasting exercise: How *predictable* is the subject of our forecast – what is the range of possible alternatives? How *malleable* is this subject – to what extent may the future be altered by our actions?

This book is about a particular sort of forecast which is enjoying a certain current vogue: a forecast of a liberal and humane future, an environmentally conscious future, a future in which social change is directed, no longer by a mechanical rationality, but rather in response to human needs. It takes four different accounts of this gentle future – *The New Liberty* by Ralf Dahrendorf, *The Coming of Post-Industrial Society* by Daniel Bell,[4] *Small is Beautiful* by E. F. Schumacher[5] and *Economics and the Public Purpose* by J. K. Galbraith[6] – and asks whether the description of the future that may be pieced together from these books is feasible, and what might be done to help it come about.

2 Choosing a Future

The authors of the four books are not merely making simple predictions, they are also saying something about the malleability of the future. They share the view that we are now at a point in history at which we are newly able to choose the direction of social development; up till now the pattern of change in societies has been determined by economic and social and technical forces beyond our control; from now on, they argue, we will be in a position to choose our direction. The process of determination to which we have until now been subject would be explained by the four authors as follows:

1. The society is subject to scarcity. Almost all of its members will wish to consume more goods to meet their basic needs for food, shelter and clothing.

2. There will therefore be a tendency to exploit available economies of scale to the fullest possible extent. The division of labour in industrial production produces more goods to meet the basic demands of the members of the society.

3. New technologies are scarce. The society is developing its technological expertise, and those technologies which are proved feasible and which *may* be employed in reaping economies of scale *will* be so used.

4. In particular, communications are sparsely provided. This poses problems for the administration and control of industrial enterprises, so the form of organisation is probably limited to some form of private ownership and individual entrepreneurial activity.

The view is of a rather mechanical determination of social patterns. This determination works in two ways. On one hand, economics at any point determines social structure in the immediate sense that the existing quantity and distribution of productive goods determines the social patterns of their employment and the consumption of their product. And on the other, present economic and social facts determine *future* economic and social conditions. It should be stressed that no one really sees determinism in such absolute terms. Societies do develop in different ways, even starting under apparently identical economic conditions; there is always some flexibility. The liberal theorists, however, conjecture that the present-day developed countries have passed some historical watershed of flexibility. In the past we could say 'things ride men', but in the passing of industrial society 'things' lose their dominion and 'society is made . . . more malleable'. The emerging society is 'a society *in charge of itself* rather than . . . restructured to suit the logic of instruments and the interplay of forces that they generate'.[7]

Bell describes this new state of man as follows:

> For most of human history, *reality was nature*, . . . then *reality became technics* . . . now *reality is primarily the social world* – neither nature nor society gives rise to a new Utopianism . . . the restraints of the past vanish with the end of [the dominion of] nature and things. (Bell, *The Coming of Post-Industrial Society*, p. 488)

This view of the malleable society relates point for point with the four-part explanation of economic determinacy in a developing industrial society.

1. Increasing wealth means less unrequited need for goods to satisfy basic needs; this does not mean that demands for increased consumption cease – possibly quite the opposite – but, basic needs being satisfied, they may be much more diverse, and there is greater discretion as to which are met. (Hence, for example, choices between leisure and consumption.) We should note that this is not a question only of wealth, but also of its distribution – it might be argued that our society, in spite of its wealth, still has members whose basic needs are unmet. But without overstressing this point, we can see that poverty no longer imposes an automatic requirement for growth in the provision of a highly defined range of basic goods.

2. As technologies develop, advantages of scale accrue to increasingly small productive units. We might consider, for example, that the thermal efficiency of the largest electricity generating set could now probably be achieved by very much smaller ones, so that while the National Grid was necessary forty years ago to provide a particular level of service, if we were to start from scratch, we could achieve the same or higher levels of

service from much smaller (city-sized?) units. (Other examples abound in the transport and manufacturing systems.[8]) The automatic tendency towards increasing scale and division of labour over time is thus greatly weakened.

3. Technologies are no longer scarce. Instead of social shortcomings demanding technical solutions we now often find multiple technologies chasing scarce applications. (A recent study identifies 178 distinct unconventional passenger transport systems, all in some stage of research or development; only a tiny fraction of these will ever be evaluated at full scale, and conceivably none of them might ever come into general use.[9]) This is particularly significant since alternative technologies may permit alternative patterns and proportions of use of factors of production for the same job. As an example here, we might cite the group technology experiments in motor manufacturing which produce cars almost as efficiently as the conventional assembly line techniques – increasing capital to provide more humane use of labour. So the existence of a technology may no longer determine the pattern of production.

4. Finally, the development of new 'control' technologies may substitute for some of the above factors. Improvements in transport, telecommunications and data-handling may produce the opportunities for different types or uses of organisations. The emerging innovatory forms of social organisation – worker participation in management, for example – do not require these new technologies; many have roots in the nineteenth century. But certainly the control technologies do facilitate such innovation. The prevalent notion of determination applied to organisational form is Weber's: a progressive bogging down in the forms and foibles of a bureaucracy that ramifies to meet the needs of an ever more complex industrial society. The control technologies may provide an avenue of escape by providing for more flexible adjustment among interacting groups through increased information flow.

This argument is not stated explicitly and in its entirety by any of the liberal theorists, but its components are all present, as Chapter 2 will demonstrate, in some form or other. And from these points may be derived all the themes that characterise this view of the future – increasing leisure time, decreasing working day, increases in the service sector, smaller units of production, diversification of consumption.

3 Inertial Mechanisms and Social Change

Is the future really now as malleable as this argument suggests? Even if we are now less determined by economic and technological conditions, we may still be constrained by our culture and social organisation. We can specify three inertial mechanisms which tend to limit the malleability of the future.

Change in society is a process of accretion. Social innovations add to the body of existing conditions just as new growths only add to the existing bulk of a coral reef; the replication of language, family, complex organisational structures over time is an easily recognisable example of this phenomenon. Capital formation is a suggestive concept here; social infrastructure – language, cities, transport and communications structures – in some sense involves enormous capital investment, made with immensely long (centuries) time horizons. And replacement of this capital is incremental: in those sectors with the longest investment time horizons (established cities?) replacement may be at the rate of fractions of a per cent per year. The existence of such an infrastructure obviously leads to a drag resisting social innovation. To revert to the transport example cited above, of the large number of competing new technologies for mass long-distance ground transport, there is a high probability that *none* of these will be employed in the next thirty years, because of the existing capital stock in railways and the necessity for staggered incremental investment in its maintenance. Specifically, in this book, we shall be investigating the prediction – which is in some cases only a prescription – of a change in the pattern of consumption in the developed world, from a material, individualist or household basis to a less material, communal or social basis. Now the existence of a large amount of laid-down capital in the form of a stock of dwellings which are designed for a single nuclear family, laid out in a diffuse settlement pattern, places a limit on the possibility of a radical change in the methods we use to meet our needs. Change is possible, but the capital costs are high; the existence of the capital in this form must tend to maintain us on our course of increasing consumerism.

Apart from the 'historical investment' aspect of social structure, some institutions contain mechanisms for maintaining themselves unchanged in a changing environment. Cultural forms may evolve so that – like genes, which can be viewed as selecting so as to maximise the probability of their own survival across generations[10] – they have an inherent tendency to replicate themselves over time. It may be that consumerism is an example of such a self-replicating structure; the notions of personal possession, together with the observation that others have more personal possessions, may themselves determine the individual's striving for further possessions. A member of a society which has no concept of personal property desires no property, but the concept has an inherent logic such that, once introduced, it is difficult to reverse the cultural forms and processes that it encourages. Even if, as some of our group of writers argue, the environmental circumstances which previously enforced the pursuit of material wealth are no longer pressing, the pursuit of material wealth may still continue unabated.

A third reason for stability over time is the generally incremental nature of most decision-taking. Most governmental decisions represent only marginal alterations of current conditions. We can recognise a number of reasons for this. First and foremost it is because of the institutional context of policy-making: policies are chosen according to established procedures, using established criteria and indicators for the failure or success of provisions, within institutions which have established objectives. But apart from this positive recognition that the majority of policies are only incremental changes from existing conditions, it can be argued that policy-makers *ought* only to think in terms of incremental changes.[11] After all, we know (in principle) the results of current policies, so we can probably predict the results of *small* changes – and if their results turn out to be too disastrous we can always go back to the previous position. While we have decision-making procedures which are dominated by concerns with budgetary control (and particularly with the expectation that one year's budgetary allocation is the main determinant of the next) and while these decisions are made in the context of a hierarchical and highly subdivided structure (and hence highly constrained by established performance criteria), we can expect government to have only an inertial effect on social structure. The implementation of radical policies can only be hindered by the incremental tendency of government.

4   The Purpose of this Book

This book is a record of research in progress. When the first three chapters were written the author had no very clear position on the questions they ask. The empirical research that forms the substance of the book was informed by a number of simple questions: How has the sectoral pattern of employment changed over the last two decades? In what ways have the nature of the jobs changed? How have consumption patterns altered over the period? Out of the answers to these questions came the particular view of the likely future that is suggested here; the book describes the author's sequence of investigation. The result of this way of organising the writing is inevitably an untidy book. The first half of the book opens broad issues which are only considered rather narrowly in the second.

The justification for publishing the book in this form is that it presents findings which challenge, in some important respects, the conventional view of the future of developed economies. It looks at the factual basis of the liberals' view of the future and finds evidence of trends which run quite contrary to their predictions and prescriptions. In particular, careful examination of changes in employment and consumption patterns in the United Kingdom over the last twenty-five years reveals, not the gradual emergence of a 'service economy', but its precise opposite. Where we would expect, according to the current dogma, to find a considerable rise in the consumption of services, we find instead a remarkable fall in service consumption as a proportion of the total. Instead of buying services, households seem increasingly to be buying – in effect *investing* in – durable goods which allow final consumers to produce services for themselves. A large proportion of the growth in service employment over the period can be explained not by service consumption, but by the need of manufacturing industry for technically trained personnel, managers and salesmen, for the efficient production of consumer durables. This is in effect a *self*-service economy, with paid employment concentrated in technical and managerial occupations in manufacturing industry, while services are produced outside the formal economy, through direct labour, using capital machinery installed in the household. And we have every reason for expecting this trend to continue, since it is driven by two economic processes whose direction we cannot expect to vary: technical innovation leading to cheaper and improved capital machinery on one hand; and rising labour costs on the other.

The book makes a prediction which is at variance with the pronouncements of the four liberal theorists; the image of the future projected in this book is in many respects less humane and caring than theirs. Can we do anything to avoid the self-service economy? Is the future we predict a malleable one? The book does not really attempt to answer the question even though it urgently needs answering. Ultimately, the purpose of this book is just to pose a question: have we built up such inertia in our progress towards the self-service economy that its full and rather unpleasant development is inevitable, or is there some way in which we might influence our future towards an improving society? The following discussion will establish the existence of the problem, but provide no more than hints as to the answer.

CHAPTER ONE

THE HINGE OF HISTORY

1   The Second Coming of Post-Industrial Society?

There is a widespread suspicion that we are at some unique historical crossroads, that we are at the end of the old undeviating path of economic development, that 'the subject of history has changed'.[1]

> In the advanced societies of the world, with their market economies, open societies and democratic politics, a dominant theme appears to be spent, the theme of progress in a certain, one-dimensional sense. The new theme . . . is no longer expansion but what I shall call improvement, qualitative rather than quantitative development. (Dahrendorf, *The New Liberty*, p. 14)

This assumes a particular view of the historical process, a view in which societies must inevitably progress through a given series of stages which form the path of development. Dahrendorf's 'new theme' was earlier canvassed as the ultimate stage in one such theory of history, that contained in W. W. Rostow's *The Stages of Economic Growth*.[2]

Societies, according to Rostow's conceptualisation, are at first 'traditional' – not necessarily unchanging but at least stable, with an upper limit to output per head, and with little social mobility. Gifted individuals recognise the possibilities for the application of systematic knowledge and organisation to agricultural and industrial production, and the benefits that such economic progress may bring, so that isolated ghettoes of 'modernisation' grow up alongside the traditional economic institutions. As these 'enclaves of modern activity' grow past a certain critical size, the benefits of modernisation become obvious to a wide section of the community, and the economy 'takes off' into sustained growth. In the next stage the economy 'drives toward maturity', applying technological expertise to an ever-wider range of economic activities, until it reaches the 'mature' stage of 'high mass consumption' which may be identified by the predominantly urban settlement pattern and the widely-distributed affluence of the populations of Western Europe and the United States.[3]

Rostow is, however, reluctant to commit himself to a prediction about the nature of the next and ultimate stage. He poses a number of alternatives:

> Will man fall into secular spiritual stagnation . . . ? Will men learn to conduct wars with just enough violence to be good sport – and to accelerate capital depreciation – without blowing up the planet? Will the exploration of outer space offer an adequately interesting and expensive outlet for resources and ambitions? Or will man, converted *en masse* into a suburban version of an eighteenth-century country gentleman, find in some mixture of the equivalent of hunting, shooting and fishing, the life of the kind and the spirit, and the minimum drama of carrying forward the human race, sufficient frontiers to keep for life its savour? (Rostow, *The Stages of Growth*, p. 91)

He does, however, make a definite prediction for the short-run future of the United States. Its destiny is to be found not in 'the further diffusion of consumer durables', but in the provision of 'social overhead capital' – schools, medical facilities, welfare benefits.[4] This is the sort of view espoused by the four authors (Bell, Galbraith, Dahrendorf and Schumacher) we are to discuss in this book – that at this point in history the developed world is entering the new stage of 'improvement'.

But this is not the first historical era in which social scientists have proposed that economic growth be replaced by qualitative improvement. Indeed, Dahrendorf himself quotes briefly from the following passage from John Stuart Mill's *Principles of Political Economy*.[5]

> I cannot . . . regard the stationary state of capital and wealth with the unaffected aversion so generally manifested towards it by political economists of the old school. I am inclined to believe that it would be, on the whole, a very considerable improvement on our present condition. I confess I am not charmed with the ideal of life held out by those who think that

the normal state of human beings is that of struggling to get on; that the trampling, crushing, elbowing, and treading on each other's heels, which form the existing type of social life, are the most desirable lot of human kind, or anything but the disagreeable symptoms of one of the phases of industrial progress. . . . the best state for human nature is that in which, while no one is poor, no one desires to be richer, nor has any reason to fear being thrust back, by the efforts of others to push themselves forward. . . . the stationary state of capital and population implies no stationary state of human improvement. (Mill, *Political Economy*, pp. 453-4)

We might note that the first edition of *Political Economy* was published in 1848, the 'Year of Revolutions', three years before the Great Exhibition which Rostow uses to mark Britain's entry into the stage of 'maturity', and nearly ninety years before, on Rostow's reckoning, Britain reached the stage of 'high mass consumption'.[6]

In the passage quoted above, Mill suggests that positive benefits come from the cessation of growth. Does he do so simply as an attempt to reconcile himself to a steady state that is both inevitable and imminent?

It must always have been seen, more or less distinctly, by political economists, that the increase of wealth is not boundless . . . that at the end of what they term the progressive state lies the stationary state . . . this ultimate goal is at all times near enough to be fully in view; that we are always on the verge of it, and that *if we have not reached it long ago it is because the goal itself flies before us.* The richest and most prosperous countries would very soon attain the stationary state if no further improvement were made in the productive arts, and if there were a suspension of the overflow of capital from those countries into the uncultivated or ill-cultivated regions of the earth. (Mill, *Political Economy*, p. 452, my emphasis)

Mill is clearly not predicting the near approach of the stationary state; on the contrary, if he were to assume either continued 'improvement in the productive arts' or foreign investment, which he must surely have done at that point in the development

of Britain, he would predict that such predictions were prema-
ture. Certainly the progress of wealth according to Mill is
bounded, but it only necessarily meets that bound when
productive invention is exhausted,[7] and if the potential for
invention is limitless, then, like the highest number, the bound to
opportunities for growth is infinitely distant. Mill may well have
been driven into his contemplation of the stationary state by the
supposed law of the 'tendency of profits to a minimum' but in the
two chapters preceding his discussion of the stationary state,[8] he
clearly refutes the suggestion that it is an immediate prospect for
Britain. His advocacy of the stationary state is purely partisan, a
reflection of his politics, and owes nothing to an expectation of
its imminent or unavoidable arrival.

2 Growth or Stability: an Antediluvian Debate

Mill's espousal in the 1840s of that apparently 1970s phenomenon, zero-growth economics, was by no means the first. The
debate between the proponents of economic growth and those of
qualitative improvement as a goal for policy is echoed in even the
very earliest economic writings. We can choose examples,
working backwards from Mill.[9] At the end of the eighteenth
century in France, we come upon a group of economists known
collectively as 'Physiocrats', best known of whom is François
Quesnay. Their intention was to restore stability to the social
structure of France, which had been upset by the industrial
expansion under Louis XIV's minister, Colbert, and the subsequent disastrous monetary experiments carried out by the
Scottish economist John Law in 1719 and 1720. The economics of
this school, as embodied in Quesnay's writings, constitute a
blueprint for a return to the certainties of a somewhat idealised
view of the medieval economic system. Quesnay explained his
proposed economic structure by means of his 'Tableau
Economique' – in fact, a close equivalent to the modern 'input-
output table'. The 'Tableau' specified yearly flows of payments
and commodities between three economic groups: 'productive'
workers – in modern terms, primary producers, farmers and
miners; 'sterile' workers, who transform the primary products –
that is, they manufacture goods; and 'proprietors', who consume
the surplus – leaving just enough to reproduce the working

capital for the following year. The crucial notion of value, which determines the size of the payments between the classes and thus the overall level of economic activity, is the medieval notion of the just price; as Aquinas has it, 'Those who govern the state should determine the just price of marketable commodities with due consideration of time and space' – the state was to maintain stability by determining the payments to farmers and artisans at rates that would guarantee their material subsistence and replace their capital.

The Physiocrats had an immediate forerunner in eighteenth-century France. Consider the following:

> The needs of a State grow, like the wants of individuals, less from any real necessity than from the increase of useless desires . . . sometimes the State would gain by not being rich, and apparent wealth is more burdensome than poverty itself would be. . . . Governments may hope to keep people in stricter dependence by giving them with one hand what they take away with the other. . . . The duty [of Governments] is not . . . to fill the granaries of individuals and thus grant them a dispensation from labour, but rather to keep plenty so within their reach that labour is always necessary and never useless for its acquisition. (J. J. Rousseau, *On Political Economy*)

Here again, we find the same economic outlook, the view that needs are essentially limited, that the purpose of economic activity is not the mere accumulation of wealth, but rather the maintenance of sober and useful occupations, and that this maintenance should be the goal of economic activity.

These views have their origin in medieval canon law. The reason that the state should 'determine the just price', as Aquinas has it, is its function as the ultimate arbiter of 'fair exchange' (*commutatio*), which is the proper basis for economic relations. 'Such exchanges are natural, that is, rightful; they are performed on the basis of commutative justice, value for value, equality of exchange, without loss to one nor gain to the other, but to the benefit of both, since those transactions enable them to satisfy their needs.'[10] This satisfaction of needs is the essence of the matter: *commutatio* in Aquinas' economics is to be set against *negotiatio*, exchange, not for needs but for profit. *Negotiatio* involves the attempt to sell goods at a higher price than that paid by the vendor: while the gain may reflect only the vendor's living and business expenses, it may alternatively reflect an 'unjust' profit, and is therefore to be considered unnatural. Furthermore, Aquinas stresses that where *negotiatio* involves foreign trade there are further problems; foreign traders bring foreign *mores* which upset the carefully established equilibrium and raise the possibility of higher material consumption levels to the populace. Greed for money replaces modest ambition for material sufficiency.

Aquinas' economic categories take their origin from those of Aristotle and Plato. Aristotle distinguishes two separate economic processes, *oiconomike* (household management) and *chrematistike* (the pursuit of wealth). He writes:

> The art of household management is not identical with the art of getting wealth, for the one uses the material which the other provides . . . household management attends more to men than to the acquisition of material things, and to human excellence rather than to that excellence of property which we call wealth. (Aristotle, *Politics*, 1256a, 1259b)

Aristotle's position is itself a development of Plato's: 'poverty results from increase of man's desires, not from diminution of his property'. For Plato and Aristotle, the policy of the state should be determined by considerations of *chrematistike* only as far as was necessary to provide a sufficiency for modest needs, after which the pursuit of wealth could give none but illusory benefits:

> A good man may make the best even of poverty and disease and the other ills of life; but he can only attain happiness under the opposite conditions. . . . This makes men imagine that external goods are the cause of happiness, yet we might just as well say that a brilliant performance on the lyre was to be attributed to the instrument and not to the skill of the performer. (Aristotle, *Politics*, 1332a, 18–28)

In otherwords, *oiconomike*, sound management of a stable society, is the ultimate goal; not material growth but personal improvement.

Of course, Athens in the third century B.C. also had its proponents of growth as an end in itself. Aristotle and Plato were concerned with these issues in order to contradict the economic doctrines of the Sophists, which were what we now call mercantilist – concerned to promote the expansion of trade. A surviving economic policy document, *Ways and Means to Increase the Revenues of Athens*, believed to date from approximately 355 B.C., outlines some strategies.[11] It stresses the importance of extra-economic management for merchants – it suggests state investment in the transport infrastructure, harbour improvements, and state warehouses, and even the hiring-out of state-owned slaves and of state-owned ships for commercial purposes. Apart from the absence of emphasis on technical change, this is closely akin to a growth strategy which might be adopted by a modern state. So in Plato's and Socrates' opposition of *oiconomike* to the Sophists' *chrematistike*, we can see a clear counterpart of our opposition of social improvement to economic growth.

With only a slight excess of pedantry, we can put this debate in literally antediluvian terms. Consider Lord Robbins' view of the nature of the economic problem:[12] 'We have been turned out of Paradise. We have neither eternal life nor unlimited means of gratification.' Our former home was a place of ease and plenty, says this view, and we must now work to live only because we have been turned out of it. This is Hesiod's Paradise, however – the 'golden age', and not the Garden of Eden – for we are explicitly told 'the Lord God took the man and put him in the Garden of Eden to till it and to keep it', and also, before the Fall, Adam is ordered: 'Be fruitful and multiply, and fill the earth, and subdue it; and have dominion over the fish of the sea and the birds of the air and over every living thing that moves upon the earth'. Work, according to the Biblical account, is clearly not a consequence of economic scarcity, and thus to be made unnecessary by the promotion of plenty, but rather a natural and desirable activity; in this view 'pie in the sky' would be accompanied by at least part of a day's work – perhaps in environmental maintenance and ecological management.

It is possible to draw out of this historical discussion two quite different views of what economics is all about. It is difficult to decide on names for these views; Aristotle's names for the two processes *oiconomike* and *chrematistike* could serve; Aquinas' *com-*

mutatio and *negotiatio* similarly, but in the interests of simplicity, we shall follow Dahrendorf's usage of 'improvement' for the former and adopt 'growth' for the latter. Growth theorists view the economic process as the exploitation of resources to placate insatiable needs, whereas improvement theorists visualise the economic problem more as one of harbouring resources and managing needs. The growth ideology has wealth and its increase as an ultimate aim, and sees the art or science of economics as a neutral tool, a means to wealth, whereas the improvement ideology ascribes to objects only their inherent use value, and sees the subject matter of economics to be as much in ends as in means. The one sees work as necessary and evil, only undertaken because of the extrinsic benefit gained by it; the other as intrinsically satisfying, a necessary part of good life. We must not be tempted to draw too distinct a difference between them; there are many blurred edges, and most people's economic ideologies will in real life contain elements from both sides of the divide. But nevertheless, there is a certain internal consistency to each of them, and we shall use the two categories throughout this book as if they were truly opposing monolithic ideologies. Certainly, the four social theorists we shall be discussing in the following chapter do seem to fall very neatly into the 'improvement' category.

3 Growth or Improvement: a Political Question?

The issue we are addressing in this chapter is that of whether we really have arrived at some special historical juncture, a 'hinge in history' as Dahrendorf and the other improvement theorists tell us. Either there has been some objective change in the dynamics of social development – that is, the economic and technical forces impelling change in developed countries are in some qualitative way different now to those hitherto – or else our present-day improvement theorists are simply articulating the same social and political values and assumptions which produced the improvement theories of the earlier writers we discussed in the previous section.

As for the first possibility, there may at first sight appear to have been such a change introduced by the Club of Rome through the 'Limits to Growth' thesis, but of the four theorists we are to consider, only Schumacher accepts the Limits thesis.[13] Dahrendorf indeed mentions the thesis, but only to dismiss it as nothing more than an impressionistic warning.[14] As for the converse thesis, that we have reached the 'end of scarcity' and that therefore further growth is not impossible but simply unhelpful, while each of the writers feels that present levels of production of material goods are sufficient to meet the reasonable needs of the population of the developed world, this is not the satiation which is the goal of *chrematistike*, but merely an adequacy, which is the end of *oiconomike*. These writers do not believe in the imminent and inevitable end of growth any more than Mill did; they rather believe, like Mill, and Quesnay and Rousseau and Aquinas and Aristotle and Plato, that growth in the quantity of material consumption is not the aim of the good life, but rather that the goal is the improvement of its quality.

Now, without trespassing too far on the substance of this book, some people hold a number of what they consider to be good reasons for wanting further economic growth. They may feel that they themselves, or others for whom they are concerned, have insufficient command of material goods at present; or they may feel that economic growth is a useful mechanism for taking the heat out of social conflict; or they may feel that growth enables some other desirable end, such as improvements in the organisation of the workplace. How do our improvement theorists differ from these liberal-minded men who still put their faith in further growth?

Here we must voice an unkind suspicion. Consider: one's political position is determined in part by perceptions of what is possible, and in part by judgements of what actions are allowable, and of what results are desirable. All of them are conditioned, to a major degree, by one's position in the world, by class and class background. Now take the status of our four authors – they are advisers to Presidents and great state corporations, academics at the pinnacles of their profession, senior international civil servants or diplomats. These are men of power, but a particular sort of power, not based on personal wealth, but on their own expertise, and on their use of this expertise at a critical point in a political system. They are presumably men divorced from any personal material needs, and for whom the abstract functions of material possession – the

acquisition of status and self-confidence – must be quite irrelevant. Could it be that their personal abstraction from material
concerns has influenced their rejections of materialist economic
philosophy? Certainly, considering the professions of the earlier
writers, we do see some similarity; a high executive of the East
India Company, a Minister of the French State, a great
medieval churchman, a revered teacher in a slave-owning Greek
state – again, men abstracted from many normal material
concerns.

If this is going too far, we can at least put the same
considerations in a rather weaker form. This same debate of
growth versus improvement has continued for at least the last
two-and-a-half millenia. We have no evidence that the conditions under which the argument is entered are in any critical
way different now from any other time during that period. So we
must leave open the possibility that this 'new theme of history'
broached by our four authors is no more than a further
recurrence of one side of an ancient political argument. We do
not need to invent, in Schumacher's term, a 'Buddhist Economics', since we have one already in the economics that has
descended to us from third century B.C. Athens via medieval
canon law.[15]

CHAPTER TWO

SOME POST-INDUSTRIAL THEMES

1 Four Modern Improvement Theorists

This chapter outlines the views of the four theorists whose positions we shall adopt in order to formulate the 1970s version of the improvement ideology. In the case of each author, one book is adopted as a focus for discussion.

1.1 *Dahrendorf: 'The New Liberty'*

Its subtitle, *Survival and Justice in a Changing World*, immediately faces us with a problem. Justice and liberty may be – in a world of scarcity – opposed to each other; a 'just' distribution of resources may only be achievable at the cost of liberty. To adopt liberty as a goal under conditions of scarcity may lead to the perpetuation or aggravation of an existing social injustice. The pursuit of social improvement instead of economic growth might well lead to costs in terms of Dahrendorf's other stated goals, at least in the short-term.[1] Dahrendorf is at pains to stress that his adoption of liberty as the primary goal is to be explained by his own personal experience of a totalitarian regime; once basic material needs have been satisfied, he would argue the need to protect individual liberty. The central theme of the book is given as a motto taken from the passage in Mill's *Political Economy*, quoted in the previous chapter: 'The stationary state of capital and population implies no stationary state of human improvement'. But the liberty that Dahrendorf hopes to achieve is certainly not the 'liberty of the poor man to dine at the Ritz'; it is clear that his position is a recognition of the *feasibility* of the pursuit of liberty – extending the range of possibility of genuine choice among alternative life styles – in contrast to the growing *difficulty* of economic expansion. Growth, we may infer, is not necessarily a bad thing in itself, but we cannot easily maintain it, and anyway, improvement (that is, increasing liberty) is more pertinent to the problems of individuals in developed societies.

The central problem is how to bring about the 'improving

society'. Dahrendorf suggests that the locus of political struggle has moved from the conflict between the proletariat and the bourgeoisie, to the conflict between, on the one hand, the employees and owners of oligopolistic firms which have enough power to influence their own markets and which can, in the last event, maintain or even improve the wages of employees in the face of inflation by passing increased cost on to consumers, and on the other, the rest of the working population who have no such power and thus lose ground in an inflation. The 'industrial classes', to use Dahrendorf's term, are then the party for continued economic growth; from where will come support for the improving society? Dahrendorf has no definite answer: 'I hope nobody will expect me', he says, 'to come up with a great surprise and produce . . . the *classis ex machina*, the saving social class'. He does, however, have three suggestions for the provenance of support for the new society. First, he suggests that some members of the current ruling establishment in developed countries may 'explore new ways and entertain somewhat unorthodox ideas'. However, given that he suggests the Club of Rome as his example, we might not take this suggestion very seriously.[2] The second suggestion is that workers in the 'media', with their concern about liberty, might ally themselves with the more progressive members of the establishment – but Dahrendorf also points out that their effect is more typically to confuse and to cross-pressure rather than to give any constructive leadership. Third, he suggests that those most involved in the student unrest will at some time in the future reach positions of power, and will then lead us towards the improving society, though again we could have doubts about the survival of the ideals of youth into middle age.

Another central issue for Dahrendorf is the liberation of the individual from the bondage of bureaucracy:

> An agenda for recovering public control and individual rights from bureaucracies, while preserving their service for the solution of problems of scale and citizenship is one of the primary tasks of the search for a new liberty. It involves more than one tough decision; decentralisation of hitherto centralised functions; citizen participation in communities and organisations; a reconsideration of systems of tenure for

administrative officers; the reduction of hierarchical structures by a strengthening of task and team orientations; and other efforts along the line of relaxing bureaucratic rigidity. (Dahrendorf, *The New Liberty*, p. 41)

Again, we should note the agnostic position taken by Dahrendorf. Small is not necessarily beautiful ('preserving their services for the solution of problems of scale') – the requisite size of an organisation is dependent on the specifics of its circumstances, and if there are benefits of scale, and the loss of liberty is acceptably small, then the large institution may be justified.

So far, we have talked mainly in abstract terms about Dahrendorf's plea for new social goals. He also is concerned to make his argument more concrete by including consideration of a number of specific changes for the improvement of the life styles of individuals. He considers, for example, the workplace:

There are specific problems here of the division of labour and how to relax its rigidities. Workplaces do not have to be as overdetermined as they often are. Experiments in group cooperation even on the assembly line, in a wider involvement of employees in the organisation of work, in industrial participation, are promising. (Dahrendorf, *The New Liberty*, p. 75)

With this comes a bundle of liberal proposals for improving quality of life; continuing education, available as of right to all members of the society and to be taken at any stage of life; income maintenance to free individuals from the sort of economic insecurity which might lead them to desire economic growth above improvement; more leisure, and a wider range of opportunities for enjoying it (including taking second jobs); and most important, liberating individuals (particularly housewives) from the necessity of doing some particular and undesired job.

Dahrendorf sums up his argument as follows:

Whereas the central institutions of the expanding society were economic, those of the improving society are political, that is public, general and open. . . . This then is what the improving society is about: a new lease of life for men boxed up in the unnecessary cubicles of an inherited division of labour, based on an economy of good husbandry, and brought about by a political organisation in which the revolt of the individual is reconciled with the need for recognising both the reality of organisation and the utility of wider spaces. (Dahrendorf, *The New Liberty*, p. 81)

He holds that we are less subject to economic determination than formerly, and makes a plea that we should take advantage of our wider horizons to provide a more humane society.

1.2   Bell: 'The Coming of Post-Industrial Society'[3]

Bell's thesis is that the next thirty to fifty years will see in the developed countries the emergence of the post-industrial state, the skeleton of which already exists in the United States. Bell's notion of the post-industrial state may perhaps be best defined by inclusion. In the post-industrial state the most important econ-omic product comes from the tertiary sector (Bell also uses 'quarternary' and 'quinary' for the latter members of the following list) including transport, public utilities, trade, finance, insurance, real estate, health, education, research, government and recreation. (See Bell's table 1.1.) The most significant occupational categories are the professions, engineers, tech-nicians and scientists, the society is dependent on information and abstract analysis for its maintenance, its critical activity is the codification and assimilation of knowledge, and the crucial power variable is the control of knowledge.

He is particularly careful to stress that his scope is much less universal than Rostow's stages of growth thesis, which he dismisses as a caricature. He explicitly disclaims the convergence hypothesis – the 'remarkable parallel' between the patterns of development of the United States and the U.S.S.R.[4] He does however assert that both capitalist and communist states are undergoing similar changes in their social structure; for an industrial society (this pretty much resembles Rostow's stage of 'high mass consumption') in either sort of state, the central process of structural change, the 'axial principle' is economic growth whether controlled by the state or by private investment decision; whereas, in the following stage of 'post-industrial' society the axial principle is the acquisition and codification of theoretical knowledge, and power resides in the possession – and in the person of the possessors – of this knowledge. There are two intertwined reasons for this change. The first is essentially organisational:

> . . . the scientific and technological revolution cannot be led by the working class . . . the stratification system of the new society will emphasise the dominance of the professional and technical classes . . . if the production and maintenance of the scientific mastery of the future society requires the presence of a highly trained research elite, supported by a large technical staff, does not all this define the attributes of a new potential ruling class? (Bell, *The Coming of Post-Industrial Society*, p. 109)

However this is not in itself a sufficient explanation; it does not tell us how or why the new elite will gain control from the old. Bell's answer, the second reason for the growing 'centrality of theoretical knowledge', is that the transfer of power is enabled – or enforced – by a change in the needs of the society. Now here we encounter a worrying inconsistency in the book; the section of the 'Coda' which asks the question: 'Has the economic problem been solved?' answers somewhat in the negative, and yet the whole drift of the argument of the book outside these few pages points in precisely the opposite direction, at least as regards material consumption.[5] In the Introduction, Bell quotes approvingly the arguments of Colin Clark in *The Conditions of Economic Progress*[6] to the effect that the needs of developed societies are increasingly for the provision of immaterial services, and this theme – as for instance in the title of the second chapter 'From Goods to Services: The Changing Shape of the Economy' – extends throughout his book; so he clearly does believe in at least the end of material scarcity as a problem for the individual. He does, however, contrast these immaterial personal needs with a set of newly emerging social needs; for the protection of the environment, for the accounting of the indirect social costs and benefits of individual human actions, for the public provision for needs which could not be met by private individuals or corporations. These newly-dominant requirements for managerial services and for their provision on a societal rather than an individual basis lead, to continue Bell's argument, to the

emergence of new decision-making criteria – the dominant process of changes from the 'economising mode' to the 'sociologising
mode'.

> The 'economising' mode is oriented to functional efficiency
> and the management of things (and men treated as things).
> The sociologising mode establishes broader social criteria, but
> it necessarily involves the loss of efficiency, the reduction of
> production, and other costs that follow the introduction of
> non-economic values. . . .
>
> We now move to a communal ethic, without that com-
> munity being, as yet, wholly defined. In a sense, the movement
> away from governance by political economy to governance by
> political philosophy – for that is the meaning of the shift – is a
> turn to non-capitalist modes of social thought. And this is the
> long-run historical tendency in Western society. (Bell, *The
> Coming of Post-Industrial Society*, pp. 42, 43, 298)

In other words, Bell predicts that economic growth will be
replaced as the goal for social development by social improvement. But the argument leaves us with two problems: granted
that the knowledge elite is increasingly important to the wealth of
an increasingly technologically-oriented society – but why
should it become politically dominant, why should its members
become Dahrendorf's *classis ex machina*? And even if they were
thus to predominate, why should they be any less materialist and
profit-oriented than our present decision-makers?

We have already seen that the idea of improvement existed
long before our present era. These previous writers proposed
quite different strategies for the implementation of sociologising
criteria; Mill, for example, proposed that the vested interests of
ownership of capital be gradually reduced by a legal restriction
on inheritance, and that workers be involved in industrial
decision-making by the replacement of capitalist control with
workers' cooperative ownership.[7] Whether this or any other such
historical strategy was really feasible is irrelevant; the point is
that the coming dominance of the knowledge elite is just one
among a number of possibilities for the emergence of the
sociologising mode of decision-making. The knowledge elite may
indeed be 'the saving social class', but there are other candidates.

Bell does provide ample evidence of the growing size of the professional and technical workforce, and the evidence presented in the next two chapters will confirm and amplify this observation in the context of the United Kingdom. But can we identify the importance of the contribution of a body of workers directly with its exercise of influence in the decision processes of a state? Certainly, white collar workers are crucial to the performance of a modern economy, but then so are transport workers, or workers in public utilities. The knowledge elite is certainly important to the future development of societies, but the extent to which that importance will be manifested in decision power depends on a number of issues other than that importance, and in any case, will certainly vary from country to country and among different historical periods.[8] The coming dominance of the knowledge elite must, for the moment, remain problematical.

Finally, we have no very clear grounds for assuming that even were the knowledge elite to come to power, it would indeed adopt the values of the improving society. Certainly, to the extent that doctors and teachers and social workers have power we might safely assume that they might introduce non-economic decision criteria, at least in relation to their own specialities. But since, as we shall see, the majority of those in Bell's knowledge elite category are involved more or less directly in the process of the production of material goods, and since the main purpose of their involvement in production is precisely to enlarge the tangible economic product, we could hardly expect such a class, once in power, to adopt non-economic decision criteria. It *might* do . . . but we have no grounds for presuming that it would.

So we are left in the end with two quite separate threads of argument. We have the observation, which is endorsed by the findings discussed in later chapters, that employment in certain categories of white-collar job has increased, and a prediction that this trend will continue. And we have a further prediction that this 'knowledge elite' will emerge as the class possessing both the determination and the resources to implement a programme of social improvement as opposed to economic growth. This second thread seems rather weak, since it depends ultimately on the nature of the newly-emerging needs in the developed world; if these new needs are in fact non-material, and only to be provided for on a societal basis, then it would be credible. But we shall be arguing that on the contrary, personal consumption has become increasingly material and that on present trends provision for needs in the future will be increasingly organised on an individual material 'goods' basis and less on collective non-material 'services'.

We might summarise the book in the following five points.

From Goods to Services   The central assumption for Bell is the changing pattern of employment and consumption. Primary and secondary goods will require a decreasing labour input, and growth in production and employment will be mainly concentrated in the tertiary 'services' area.

The Coming Dominance of Knowledge   As we move the bulk of employment into the tertiary sector, labour in the primary and secondary sectors will be gradually replaced by technological expertise; this implies that one major aspect of growth in the tertiary sector will be of necessity the increasing size of education, research and information handling establishments.

The Subordination of the Firm   The private corporation bases its behaviour on its economic best interests. These are not necessarily profit maximisation, but they will certainly have something to do with the flow of funds into and out of the firm. There is, however, nothing to connect these flows of funds with the external costs of the firm's operations, and as the scope of government actions widens, private corporations will be increasingly subject to government regulation to bring the firms' actions into conformity with public policy.

More Social Planning   The previous points all suggest that government will have an increasing role to play in the post-industrial state. In order that governments may fulfil this new role adequately, we must develop new planning techniques. We will need to develop new social accounting procedures, and ways of predicting the effects of innovative policies.

A Growing Technocracy   Given this increased involvement of government in the highly technical business of social planning, Bell infers that those competent in the new social technology will necessarily gain an increasing power in government. He sees the post-industrial state as increasingly technocratic, with skills and education replacing birth, property and position as the basis of political power.

1.3   Galbraith: 'Economics and the Public Purpose'[9]

This is in direct line of descent from two of Galbraith's earlier books, *The Affluent Society* and *The New Industrial State*. Indeed, the first three-quarters of *Economics and The Public Purpose (EPP)* is very similar in content to the latter of these, so the following thumbnail sketch of Galbraith's view about present problems and future possibilities will be a combination of these. Galbraith's villain is the large public corporation, which, having no effective owner (the individual stockholder being in general powerless), chooses policy according to the needs of its own employees. And given that the employees in the corporations may be assumed to wish first to stay in the employ of the corporation, and then to rise within the corporation, the purposes of the corporation may be assumed to be two-fold – first to perpetuate its own existence, and then, if possible, to expand – and of these the first is of paramount importance. But firms in a competitive market cannot guarantee either of these things. Particularly, they may be threatened by wage demands or increasing factor costs, either of which might lead to the demise of the corporation. To avoid such situations – that is, to meet the criterion of survival – the corporation tries to dominate all the markets it is involved in – to become a monopsonist in order to control whatever costs may be controlled, and a monopolist so as to be able to pass on any costs which they cannot control (or do not wish to control, notably wages) to the consumer.

In addition to this market power, the mature corporation may also have a measure of control over consumer demand through advertising. It uses this control to regulate its own growth, producing innovative products to the specifications of its advertising executives. So Galbraith would see the basic strategy of these corporations as one of maintaining security; their behaviour is oriented entirely to safeguarding the interests of their employees. Far from 'what's good for General Motors is good for the United States', Galbraith would say that any such identity of interest can only be fortuitous. And in spite of the rhetoric of free enterprise, these mature corporations form in effect a 'planning system' – a name coined by Galbraith to emphasise the contrast with those firms still subject to the insecurity of market competition.

Maintaining this 'planning system' obviously calls for a great deal of specialist technical expertise.

> The production of standardised goods and services requires specialists who have a technical knowledge of the processes and products involved or who can contribute knowledge as to possible alteration or improvement . . . For the exercise of (market) power – product planning, to devise price and market strategies, for sales and advertising management, procurement planning, public relations and government relations . . . to perfect and guide the organisation – specialists are also needed. This is the technostructure. Not a single individual but the technostructure becomes the commanding power. (Galbraith, *EPP*, pp. 81–2)

(This grouping will, of course, be familiar to us from the discussion of similar groups by Dahrendorf and Bell.)

This argument provides a theoretical explanation for all the ills of advanced industrial societies diagnosed by the writers we have been discussing in this section. And since Galbraith is himself a liberal, he provides many of the remedies we have been examining. We need, he argues, to be emancipated from the belief that growth is in the public interest; it is certainly in the interests of the planning system that people should believe this: it is less easy to believe that it is in their own interests. One (by now familiar) tool for eradicating this belief is education:

> implicit assumptions of the modern educational system . . . make income and consumption coordinate with achievement. They hold scientific, engineering, business and legal instruction to be useful; instruction in the arts, and notably if it is creative in character, to be decorative or recreational. What serves the planning system is standard fare; the rest is justified negatively in academic oratory as something the civilised man does not neglect. Educators have a particular responsibility to see that education is not social conditioning. This means the

elimination of all distinction between useful and unuseful fields of learning, all suggestion that there is an economic standard of social achievement. (Galbraith, *EPP*, p. 227)

Once having recognised that the purposes of the planning system are not identical to the public purpose it becomes necessary to *control* the behaviour of the planning system; Galbraith suggests doing this indirectly by providing support for the market system in the shape of price maintenance, exemption of small business from anti-trust laws, extension of trade unions into the market system, upward revision of the minimum wage, and other measures. One effect of the higher prices would be increased unemployment; Galbraith proposes a guaranteed wage – yet another concept introduced to us in our previous discussions.

In fact, almost all of Galbraith's conclusions are canvassed by one or more of the writers we have been examining. We find the same observation that the planning system has outflanked socialism (see Dahrendorf, pp. 27–8).

Workers have deserted socialism . . . workers are exploited . . . but the exploitation occurs in the market system. In the planning system workers are defended by unions and the state and favoured by the market power of the employing corporation which allows it to pass the cost of wage settlement to the public. Workers in this part of the economy are, relative to those in the market system, a favoured caste. (Galbraith, *EPP*, p. 276)

and this leads us to the same issue of the need for political leadership:

. . . if there is to be any chance for the emancipation of the state there must be a political grouping that accepts the public cognizance (of the difference between the purpose of the planning system and the public purpose) and is expressly committed to the public purpose. (Galbraith, *EPP*, p. 243, my parenthesis)

and again there is no suggestion of where this leadership might come from. Eventually we also find why Galbraith uses the rather clumsy term 'planning system' to describe the mature corporations. The final chapter of the book is entitled 'Coordination, Planning and the Prospect'. It deals with the positively un-American degree of government intervention and planning that the argument has led him to. 'Planning system' is obviously used to bring home to Americans the extent to which they are already the subjects of planning. Galbraith finally points out to us the necessity of comprehensive government planning of the economy: 'planning that reflects not the planning (system's purpose) but the public purpose'.

1.4   Schumacher: 'Small is Beautiful'

While Schumacher's main thrust is somewhat different from that of the other authors, there are some common aspects, so it will be worth while to mention him here.

The basic thesis of this book is the need for a new approach to economics – a 'Buddhist Economics'. The essence of the argument is that the economics of the free market is not the appropriate mechanism for meeting the needs of individuals. For Schumacher, the appropriate values for decison-taking are the Buddhist ones of appropriateness of scale and the maximisation of individual self-fulfilment. We find in *Small is Beautiful* the same set of issues of concern about the future as in the previous examples, even though in some cases the nature of the concern is slightly different.[10]

We can see this difference in the case of education. Bell sees education as fulfilling the necessity for control and management of the post-industrial state; education for him is in effect both filter and training for the soon-to-be-dominant technocratic elite. Dahrendorf on the other hand sees education simply as a means for self-fulfilment, and Schumacher shares this view; but he goes further:

> The task of our generation . . . is one of metaphysical reconstruction. It is not as if we had to invent anything new; at the same time it is not good enough merely to revert to the old formulations. Our task – and the task of all education – is to understand the present world, the world in which we live and make our choices. (Schumacher, *Small is Beautiful*, p. 93)

Education should be, this suggests, a mechanism for smoothing the transition to the improving society.

Schumacher's attitude to the pattern of production, employment and consumption is rather more vigorously expressed than those in the other books we are discussing:

> The most striking thing about modern industry is that it requires so much and accomplishes so little. Modern industry seems to be inefficient to a degree that surpasses one's ordinary powers of imagination. Its inefficiency therefore remains unnoticed (Schumacher, *Small is Beautiful*, p. 97)

There are three separate undertones to this statement. The first (and from the context possibly unintended) is the Galbraithian assertion that most consumer durables add little to the quality of individuals' lives. The second, which he argues at length, is that the system is remarkably wasteful of resources, particularly given the disparity of consumption between the developed and under-developed worlds. But the third – and the most interesting from our point of view – is that modern industry is particularly wasteful of human beings.

> Rather less than one-half of the total population of this country is, as they say, gainfully employed, and about one-third of these are actual producers . . . (not people who tell other people what to do, or account for the past, or plan for the future) . . . in agriculture, mining, construction and industry . . . a fully employed person, allowing for holidays, sickness or other absence, spends about one-fifth of his total time on his job . . . It follows that the proportion of 'total social time' spent on actual production . . . is $3\frac{1}{2}$ per cent. (Schumacher, *Small is Beautiful*, p. 125)

Now, of course, we should not take this argument too literally; Schumacher clearly recognises the need for other activities to complement his narrowly defined 'production'. But, equally, we should accept his point that there must be a very great deal of flexibility in social arrangements given that our present material living standard is maintained by such a small proportion of the total social time.

This naturally brings us to another of our central themes; if this estimate is correct, Schumacher argues, why should we not alter social arrangements to permit more satisfactory productive job structures, even if it would mean taking up a larger proportion of social time for the same social product. Perhaps we have here a means for making manual work less alienating – Schumacher certainly uses his statistic to justify a return to craft as opposed to industrial production. Again, we have a parallel to Dahrendorf, though whereas Dahrendorf suggested merely increasing the *variety* of tasks, Schumacher proposes changing the *nature* of tasks.

2 Six Post-Industrial Themes

The discussion resolves into six themes, or topics, concerning the nature of post-industrial society. Our group of authors is agreed that these represent important issues for the future of developed countries; they are not, however, always agreed as to the significance. The following brief summary attempts to outline both areas of agreement and of disagreement. A certain amount of confusion may be caused here by the fact that the literature is in part positive (that is, it consists of statements of either 'such-and-such *will* happen' or '*given these conditions* such and such *will* happen') and in part normative ('such-and-such *should* happen'). But since in either case what we are interested in is the question of whether the suggested changes are possible, and if so, under what conditions, both may be treated in the same manner.

Politics and Change It seems to be common-ground for all our authors to see the 'planning system' in Galbraith's terms, or the 'industrial classes' in Dahrendorf's, as the main block to the transition from the 'growth' goals of industrial society to the 'improvement' goals of the post-industrial society (Bell calls this the change from 'economising' to 'sociologising' mode.) However, there does not seem to be any clear idea of how to remove the block in order to achieve the transition. Galbraith and Schumacher both feel that the key to the problem is education; but socialisation takes place out of the classroom as well as in it – we cannot expect schools to produce anti-materialists when the entire social setting of the schools is a materialist one. And following Galbraith's own arguments, we certainly cannot expect a spontaneous societal conversion to post-industrial ethics. So the issue reduces itself to this: which elite or class will lead the political struggle for changed goals? Dahrendorf rather shame-facedly produces two suggestions: either the existing political elite, with or without the communications media, or else the radical student generation/cohort of the 1960s. Neither of these suggestions seems particularly likely, and from the context, Dahrendorf himself does not put any great reliance on them. Bell suggests the developing technocratic elite for the role; he does not however specify the mechanics of transition, let alone why this elite should think it in their interest to lead such a movement.

Technocracy and Planning   Here again, all of the authors are in agreement that government planning will have an increasing part to play in the post-industrial state, and again they disagree as to precisely what this role should be. Schumacher sees the necessity for some medium-term exploratory forecasting, if only for negative 'early warning' purposes. Dahrendorf has a slightly more positive view:

> . . . the establishment of a medium term perspective within a political structure . . . must be formally related to the legitimate decision-making process, and at the same time removed from the concerns which restrict the horizon of the decision-makers. (Dahrendorf, *The New Liberty*, p. 88)

Both Dahrendorf and Schumacher have an essentially Popperian view of planning – it should help to avoid mistakes in policy-making even if it cannot be used as a tool for achieving precise social goals. Galbraith finds a positive role for planning; government planning should take over and modify the directive powers of the present 'planning system', it should entirely take over some currently private sectors, utilities, health and edu-cation, and intervene actively in the remaining 'private' sectors to support small business and supervise the dismantling of the 'planning system'.

Increasing Role and Scope of Education   This is another prediction on which all four authors agree. There is, however, no shared view of what education should be for. Dahrendorf's notion of education is entirely as a service to the individual; he sees education as having the function of making better people, and suggests a continuing access to education as of right throughout life. Galbraith and Schumacher similarly see service to the individual as one function of education; they, however, give it in addition the societal function of altering the public consciousness as part of the process of change from the goal of growth to that of improvement. Bell sees a third function of education; as a means for sifting and preparing the new technocratic elite. In spite of these differences of detail, all are agreed that the educational establishment will be considerably enlarged in the transition to post-industrial society.

Change in Consumption Patterns   A central theme of Bell's book is the increasing proportion of consumption in the services, the tertiary sector, as opposed to goods in the primary and secondary sectors. This does not, of course, mean an absolute decline in the production of primary and secondary goods, but rather that future growth in consumption will be predominantly in the tertiary sector, and that productivity will rise in the primary and secondary sectors, freeing manpower for the tertiary. Schumacher and Dahrendorf see improvement in working environments (see below) such that the distinction between work and leisure becomes blurred. Galbraith considers much of the technical innovation that encourages growth in the planning system as essentially flippant and without benefit to the individual's quality of life (consider, for example, the monogramming toaster in *The New Industrial State*); with the advent of the improving society, innovation would be determined by social needs, rather than by the planning system's imperative for expansion.

Changing Attitude to, and Conditions of, Employment   As the previous point would imply, Bell sees an increasing proportion of the working population employed in the service sectors, particularly in education, administration and research. Schumacher, Dahrendorf and Galbraith, however, see an alternative option: instead of increasing productivity in the primary and secondary sectors by automation, and hence reducing manpower, they suggest altering the working environment, even at the cost of productivity, in order to reduce alienation in the workplace.

Galbraith and Dahrendorf introduce the additional concept of the guaranteed minimum wage; Galbraith suggests this merely as a 'regularisation' of welfare payments, but Dahrendorf suggests that there is no reason that the whole population should be 'gainfully employed'. He suggests that under conditions where jobs are inherently satisfying (and hence presumably the number taking this option would be limited) there is no reason that the guaranteed income should not be considered as a constructive alternative to work.

Changing Nature and Scale of Organisations   There are two separate themes here. The first relates to the scale of the organisations: Dahrendorf and Schumacher both point to the alienation stemming from involvement in large organisations and suggest that organisation size should be the minimum compatible with fulfilling its allocated function. The other theme relates to the necessity for controlling the planning system; Bell writes of the 'subordination of the corporation' by the state, and Galbraith talks of the 'liberation of the state' from the corporation. The sentiment in the two cases is identical: the behaviour of the planning system should be constrained to bring its goals into conformity with those of the state.

*   *   *

These then are the themes which go together to make the liberal view of the future. The substance of this book is an investigation into current patterns of social change in the United Kingdom to see whether we are in fact moving in the direction that the liberal theorists suggest. But before settling down to the more empirical part of the argument, we shall consider a liberal view, and an opposing view, in a rather more concrete fashion.

CHAPTER THREE

A BUDDHIST ECONOMICS?

1 Two Fictional Futures

Schumacher proposes the development of a 'Buddhist economics' as the proper frame for debate about the future of industrial societies.

> The Buddhist point of view takes the function of work to be . . . threefold: to give man a chance to utilise and develop his faculties; to enable him to overcome his egocentredness by joining with other people in a common task; and to bring forth the goods and services needed for a becoming existence. . . . To organise work in such a manner that it becomes meaningless, boring, stultifying or nerve-racking for the worker would be little short of criminal; it would indicate a greater concern with goods than with people, an evil lack of compassion and a soul-destroying degree of attachment to the most primitive side of this worldly existence. Equally, to strive for leisure as an alternative to work would be considered a complete misunderstanding of one of the basic truths of human existence, namely that work and leisure are complementary parts of the same living process and cannot be separated without destroying the job of work and the bliss of leisure. From the Buddhist point of view, there are therefore two types of mechanisation which must be clearly distinguished: one which enhances a man's skill and power and one that turns the work of man over to a mechanical slave, leaving man in a position of having to serve the slave. (Schumacher, *Small is Beautiful*, pp. 46–7)

This view is representative of the sort of humanist values implicit in the writings of the liberal theorists. The question to be asked in this chapter concerns the relevance of these attitudes to the problem of post-industrial society. Granted that the values implicit in the Buddhist economics are attractive, how feasible, how realistic, is a programme of development based on them for a society which has hitherto adopted other, more materialist goals?

A fictional case study of Buddhist economics in action is provided by Aldous Huxley's novel *Island*.[1] The setting is the tropical island of Pala, a paradise of brotherly love and appropriate technology. We might pause here to consider its history. It starts, for our purposes, with Dr Andrew McPhail, an early-Victorian Scotsman who is summoned to the bedside of the sick Rajah of Pala; Dr McPhail at first considers his condition inoperable, but then recalls, and in desperation applies, a technique of mesmerism which he has seen described with some derision in *The Lancet*. The treatment is successful and McPhail remains in Pala as the Rajah's Prime Minister. McPhail is well versed in nineteenth-century English positivism, now tempered by respect for the 'mystic' process of hypnotism; the Rajah is a Buddhist scholar and a man of deep religious experience, who, under the influence of McPhail, is enthralled by the possibilities of Western scientific method. These two together set about transforming Pala. The first step was the control, if not the abolition, of pain through yoga and hypnotism; from there to agricultural improvement, to the setting up of 'Rothampsted-in the-Tropics', and finally to education, establishing English-language schools and bursaries for foreign study. By the mid-1950s, when the book is set, Pala is a stable society developed along the lines of Schumacher's Buddhist economics, without poverty, disease, alienation or overcrowding.

There is not space here to describe in detail Huxley's intricately worked-out Utopia, but we should mention a few of the aspects which are most relevant to our discussion. First, technology: Pala is mainly an agrarian society, but still has need for some industrial production. It needs cement for building, and so has a cement works hidden in the hills and kept running by a rota of islanders. Hydro-electric power runs the communal deep-freeze for surplus agricultural product. The ruling strategy for economic development is succinctly stated as follows:

> . . . in Pala maximum efficiency isn't the categorical impera-tive that it is with you. You think first of getting the biggest possible output in the shortest possible time. We think of human beings and their satisfactions. (Huxley, *Island*, p. 154)

and more generally:

> Lenin used to say that electricity plus socialism equals
> communism. Our equations are rather different. Electricity
> minus heavy industry plus birth control equals democracy and
> plenty. Electricity plus heavy industry minus birth control
> equals misery, totalitarianism, and war. (pp. 149–50)

This leads to the system of ownership. Pala is neither capitalist
nor socialist; in the words of its spokesman:

> Most of the time we're cooperators . . . terracing and irri-
> gation call for pooled efforts and friendly agreements. Cut-
> throat competition isn't compatible with rice growing in a
> mountainous country. Our people found it quite easy to pass
> from mutual aid in a village community to streamlined
> cooperative techniques for buying and selling and profit-
> sharing and financing. (p. 150)

But this is not sufficient to guarantee political stability; how does
Pala manage to avoid internal and external conflicts?

> . . . to begin with we don't fight wars or prepare for them.
> Consequently, we have no need for conscription, or military
> hierarchies. . . . Then there's our economic system; it doesn't
> permit anybody to become more than four or five times as rich
> as the average. That means we don't have any captains of
> industry or omnipotent financiers. Better still, we have no
> omnipotent politicians or bureaucrats. Pala's a federation of
> self-governing units, professional units, economic units – so
> there's plenty of scope for small-scale initiative and democratic
> leaders, but no place for any kind of dictator at the head of a
> centralised government. (p. 152)

And residual differences between people do not give rise to
resentment; the islanders realise that all social functions are
equally necessary, and those that perform them are hence
equally deserving of respect.

The central mechanism for this transformation of a primitive
society was education. Andrew McPhail and the Rajah first

taught the teachers, and their teaching was suffused with the Buddhist economics.

> The morality to which a child goes on from the facts of ecology and the parables of erosion is a universal ethic. . . . Conservation-morality gives nobody an excuse for feeling superior, or claiming special privileges. . . . We shall be permitted to live on this planet only for as long as we treat all nature with compassion and intelligence. Elementary ecology leads straight to elementary Buddhism. (p. 220)

But, of course, people are formed by families as well as by schools, and many individual ills may be traced to the nuclear family; so we discover the device of the Mutual Adoption Club (MAC) – the super-extended family.

> Every MAC consists of anything from fifteen to twenty-five assorted couples. Newly elected brides and bridegrooms, old-timers with growing children, grandparents and great-grandparents – everybody in the club adopts everybody else. (p. 24)

We are invited to contrast the nuclear family recipe:

> Take one sexually inept wage-slave, one dissatisfied female, two or (if preferred) three small television addicts; marinate in a mixture of Freudianism and dilute Christianity; then bottle up tightly in a four-room flat and stew for fifteen years in their own juice. (p. 24)

with the MAC:

> Take twenty sexually satisfied couples and their offspring; add science, intuition and humour in equal quantities; steep in Tantrik Buddhism and simmer indefinitely in an open pan in the open air over a brisk flame of affection. (p. 23)

Children are free to move among the alternative parents within the MAC; when they grow up they join a new MAC. In this way, we are told, the Palinese avoid personality-distorting family conflicts. This does still of course leave a residual problem, of those whose inherited personalities render them potentially anti-social. These are guided by special and psychic therapy; mountain climbing for the aggressive, cathartic dancing to relieve frustration, exercise to increase awareness of others. And finally, the *moksha*-medicine, the halucinogenic taken under strict supervision as a short-cut to mystic experience.

There is a central assumption here, an interesting analogy to the notion of 'social malleability'; on Pala the human *individual* is assumed to be malleable – we have, in Palinese, the pheno-menon of 'destiny control'. The islanders have learned to control themselves; they manage pain not with drugs, but by auto-suggestion, and having learned what anti-social behaviour patterns are, they behave otherwise. And if each man determines his own course, runs Huxley's argument, he need not worry about appeasing the Fates, or conforming to inevitable laws of social development. Oedipus is a useful stereotype for the problem of the immutability of futures; at the climax of *Island* we have the legend superbly guyed as the play *Oedipus in Pala*. A child interpreter explains how Jocasta is talked out of suicide and Oedipus out of blinding himself:

> . . . the boy and girl from Pala tell them not to be silly. After all, it was an accident. He didn't know that the old man was his father. And anyway the old man began it, hit him over the head, and that made Oedipus lose his temper. . . . And when they made him king, he had to marry the old queen. She was really his mother; but neither of them knew it. And of course all they had to do when they did find out was to stop being married. And all that stuff about marrying his mother being the reason why everybody had to die of a virus – all that was just nonsense, just made up by a lot of poor stupid people who didn't know any better. (p. 253)

Pala is possible only as long as each man owns responsibility for his behaviour among his fellows, as long as he recognises the social effects of his individual actions, and chooses his own path accordingly. Oedipus on Pala does not accept his fate, he digs better sewers instead.

This then is the liberal humanist's fable of paradise. ('What a comfort', Huxley's protagonist reflects, 'to be in a place where the Fall was an exploded doctrine.') Uplifting, certainly; but we must question whether Pala tells us anything about a feasible future for developed industrial states – and even whether Pala's values are desirable. However, before we set about this, we might think about the other side of the coin; if *Island* is the humanists' ideal, Vonnegut's *Player Piano*[2] spells out all that the humanist feels should not happen to developed societies.

Player Piano describes the United States after the Second Industrial Revolution; 'the First Industrial Revolution devalued muscle work, then the second one devalued routine mental work'. The economy is overseen by the vast EPICAC computer complex in the Carlsbad Caverns, and the political machinery of the United States is reduced to a public relations function. ('. . . thanks to the machines, politics and government lived side by side, but touched almost nowhere.') All repetitive skilled engineering jobs have been automated. We have a microcosm of this process in the person of Rudi Herz, master machinist, whose actions in turning a shaft for a fractional horsepower motor have been recorded for posterity.

> . . . this little loop in the box . . . here was Rudi as Rudi had been to his machine that afternoon – Rudi the turner-on of power, the setter of speeds, the controller of the cutting tool. This was the essence of Rudi as far as the machine was concerned, as far as the economy was concerned. . . . The tape was the essence distilled from the small polite man with the big hands, and black fingernails . . . (Vonnegut, *Player Piano*, p. 16)

Rudi himself is not at all consciously resentful of having been supplanted – if anything he rejoices in the wonder of it; a little later we find him, entirely innocent of irony, extolling the virtues of a pianola.

> 'See – see them to go up and down – just the way the feller hit 'em. Look at 'em go!' The music stopped abruptly, with the air of having delivered exactly five cents' worth of job. Rudi still shouted. 'Makes you feel kind of creepy, don't it . . . watching

them keys go up and down? You can almost see a ghost sitting there playing his heart out.' (pp. 34–5)

And it is not only manual and low-grade clerical jobs that have been automated out of existence; further technical advance encroaches increasingly on technical managerial functions. As the pool of available jobs becomes shallower, so required qualifications become higher. Even the secretary to the manager of the Ilium works, herself 'more a symbol of rank than a real help', has the requisite doctorate. For those with qualifications no higher than master's degrees, or whose specialities have been automated, and for the old or sick, there are only pensions and make-work projects.

About forty men, leaning on crowbars, picks and shovels, smoking, talking, milling about something in the middle of the pavement . . . an air of sheepishness, as though there were nothing but time in the world. . . . These were members of the Reconstruction and Reclamation Corps, in their own estimate the 'Reeks and Wrecks'. Those who couldn't compete economically with machines had their choice, if they had no source of income, of the Army or the Reconstruction and Reclamation Corps. . . . Around the bar were old men, pensioners, too old for the Army or the Reeks and Wrecks. Each had before him a headless beer in a glass whose rim was opaqued by hours of thoughtful sipping. These oldsters . . . arrived early and left late, and any other business had to be done over their heads. (pp. 28–30)

We must not imagine, however, that the poor are subject to any material deprivation. As the propagandist 'Young Engineer' reminds 'John Everyman' in a set-piece play:

John – (before the advent of automation) – did you have a twenty-eight-inch television set? Or a laundry console or a radar stove or an electronic dust precipitor? . . . did you have a social insurance package that paid *all* of your medical bills, all of your dentist bills, and provided for food, housing, clothes and pocket money for your old age? John . . . has become far richer than the wildest dreams of Caesar or Napoleon or Henry

VII . . . not with all his gold and armies could Charlemagne have gotten one single electric lamp or vacuum tube. He would have given anything to get the security and health package you have, John. But could he get it? No!

Under (automation) we've become rich beyond the wildest dreams of the past! Civilisation has reached the dizziest heights of all time! Thirty-one point seven times as many television sets as the rest of the world put together! Ninety-three per cent of all the world's electrostatic dust precipitators! Seventy-seven per cent of all the world's automobiles! Ninety-eight per cent of its helicopters! Eighty-one point nine per cent of its re-frigerators! etc. etc. (pp. 185–6)

The answer to this, in the radicals' manifesto, is already familiar to us:

. . . the engineers and managers, and bureaucrats, almost alone among men of higher intelligence, have continued to believe that the condition of man improves in direct relation to the energy and devices for using energy put at his disposal. . . . Without regard for the changes in human life patterns, ways of increasing efficiency are constantly being introduced. To do this without regard for the effects of life patterns is lawless-ness . . . men and women should be returned to work as controllers of machines, and the control of people by machines (should) be curtailed . . . the effects of changes in technology and organisation of life patterns (should be) taken into careful consideration, and the changes be withheld or introduced on the basis of this consideration. (pp. 253–5, my parentheses)

Player Piano again carried the liberal humanist, Buddhist economist, message – though here by awful warning rather than by good example. Before we proceed to consider the position more critically we might briefly note the similarity between the two books. One presents a good society, which we are invited to admire, the other a bad society which we should censure: the moral viewpoints of both authors are the same. They see the same social mechanisms at work. As technological determinism leads to Ilium, so the exercise of human free-will leads to Pala. As the exigencies of wartime production set Vonnegut's cybernetic age in train, so Huxley's islanders do without armies. Material wealth, *things*, enslave, so they are to be subordinated to human *relations* and *activities*. The theme is common to both, and is central to our group of academic liberal theorists.

But there is another, and less happy, coincidence between Huxley and Vonnegut; they are both ultimately pessimistic about the survival of the humanistic ethic. For Pala is eventually conquered by a neighbouring imperialist state, and Vonnegut's neo-Luddite insurrection fails because the population of Ilium is eventually more interested in gadgets than in liberation. This does not, however, necessarily mean that liberals are fatalistically agreed as to the ultimate destiny of mankind in the Reeks and Wrecks, for Ilium is no more than an (infernally) comic metaphor. It may well be that the use of such a metaphor is significantly misleading for our purposes – there is always the possibility that a real-life Ilium might even serve some of the humanists' purposes. In the following section we shall therefore consider some qualifications to the liberal humanist position that we have been illustrating.

2   Some Questions and Qualifications

The two examples discussed above constitute no more than a caricature of the liberal/humanist position – strong opposition to growth for its own sake, and the hope for the 'improvement' of man and his environment. The moral embedded in the two examples is clear and unexceptionable; the contrast between the two novels makes a strong case for Schumacher's Buddhist economics. But how applicable are these principles to planning for the future of the United Kingdom? In this section we will discuss some questions we should ask, in very much over-simplified and abbreviated terms. We cannot answer them here, nor can we be entirely sure that we are asking the right questions, but the discussion should give some idea of the sorts of issues we will be exploring in the following chapters.

A central tenet of the improvement approach is that growth has *no* intrinsic worth, but is simply an artifact of the planning system. Galbraith states the position as follows:

The primary affirmative purpose of the technostructure is the growth of the firm. Such growth then becomes a major purpose of the planning system, and, in consequence, of the society in which the large firm is dominant. (Galbraith, *Economics and the Public Purpose*, p. 100)

Growth suits the institutional purpose of corporations, but produces little of value, only needless elaboration on current consumption patterns (*cf* Galbraith, *The New Industrial State*). This is not an entirely acceptable position.

First of all, poverty still does exist in the developed world. In the United Kingdom, for instance, a recent estimate puts approximately thirteen million people at or below the poverty line; one reflection of this is in levels of possession of consumer durables – see Table 3.1. Almost everyone living above the lowest

TABLE 3.1*   *Possession of durable goods in the United Kingdom by income of household, 1973*

Weekly income of household (£)	% of households with						
	One car	Two or more cars	Central heating (full or partial)	Washing machine	Refrigerator	Television	Telephone
Under 10	2.7	–	19.7	28.3	35.3	76.0	8.0
Over 100	48.5	44.9	71.5	79.8	95.4	96.5	81.0
All households	45.1	8.8	38.5	66.6	77.6	93.4	43.4

* For sources and comments on tables and figures, see pp. 167–77.

level of income has access to a television set, but some of the other basic conveniences of life are not so well distributed. Now these are not, of course, necessities – people may well live happy lives without central heating or washing machines or telephones – but it is uncomfortable for a liberal writer to deny people access to these things, and the advocacy of zero-growth in the United Kingdom does imply precisely such a denial, at least for the short term. Even more substantial, however, is the possession of basic household amenities. Some social groups in the United Kingdom have limited access to facilities that are normally considered necessities. According to the General Household Survey of 1974, 30 per cent of households with a non-white head of household did not have sole use of a bath or shower – and 10 per cent of them did not have even shared use of a bath. Twenty-one per cent of these households did not even have sole use of a W.C. Clearly, in the United Kingdom, economic growth has some way to go before some of the more basic manifestations of poverty are eradicated – at least in the absence of some very substantial redistribution of property.

Secondly, it is possible that economic growth is a prerequisite of political stability. It may be that developed societies consist of groups continuously competing for more advantageous positions. In the absence of growth this can only be a zero-sum game, groups can only improve their positions at the cost of other groups.[3] Growth, then, has the function of, if not the resolution of conflict, at least its articulation; through growth conflict may be rolled forward in time, so that some groups can make gains now, and other groups may make gains later without reducing the gains of the earlier winners. The no-growth, zero-sum situation, we might predict, must be unstable since the winners in any one time period have not the material for bribing the losers with promises of gains in the future. By this analysis, zero growth must lead eventually and inevitably to the breakdown of political consensus; the survival of Ilium is inconceivable without the promise of continued growth in material consumption (even though, of course, such a promise does not guarantee survival).

There are a number of additional functions fulfilled by growth. Economic growth in the developed world may be a major mechanism for promoting better conditions in the underdeveloped world. Several recent studies suggest that either with better integration into the international economic system, or by substantial but feasible transfers of capital (which of these is deemed necessary depends on the political standpoint of the study) a large part of the 'third world' could reach present-day O.E.C.D. levels of per capita income within a few generations. Such projections are, however, based on the assumption of continued growth in the developed world.[4] Rather closer to home, in a later chapter we shall suggest that one requirement of any really feasible programme for the improvement of the quality of working life in the developed world – which is one of the central goals of our 'improvement' theorists – may be the continuation of growth.

Pala is presented in a much more flattering way than is Ilium. We feel sure that people are happer on the agrarian island than in the post-industrial metropolis. But still we cannot get away from the fact that people on Pala have fewer material goods than those in Ilium; that is acceptable for the Palanese, because they do not want telephones and televisions – but how happy would the citizens of Ilium be if they were marooned on Pala? To the extent that three of our improvement writers (Galbraith, Dahrendorf, and Schumacher) believe growth in material consumption to be of only secondary significance – and to the extent that the fourth (Bell) considers private material needs in the most developed countries to be essentially satiated – they may be misleading us in the way that the comparison of Pala with Ilium misleads us.

Pala may be, in itself, a viable society, a nineteen-fifties vision of the eventual outcome of Maoism in China perhaps, but it certainly does not stand as any kind of model for the development of Europe or North America. These societies are already too tied to the process of growth in material consumption. Pala provides many services on a communal, labour-intensive basis, and this limits the size of the social product, but the Palanese are happy because they want no more than they have. Their technology is appropriate to their resources, their culture, and their aspirations. The techniques for meeting the needs of the developed world are quite different – they are, as we shall argue later in the book, increasingly capital-intensive and based on the individual or the household. Aspirations towards higher levels of consumption are encouraged both by this individualist focus and by the wide disparities of wealth among individuals and households. To adopt Pala as our model would require changing the individualist focus to a communal one, would require a levelling of disparities of wealth, and would require a reversal of aspirations to higher consumption. So Pala is not really, in this respect, a feasible model.

Another feature of the improvement literature is the development of leisure, or at least non-work activities, as an alternative to materially-productive labour. Notions such as lifelong continuing education, permanent income maintenance, and the broader diffusion of creative artistic activity run through the four books we have been describing. But Pala's main activities smack somewhat of English arts and crafts. Though some middle-class individuals (in fact, precisely our liberal theorists) may certainly be happy to exist on bread and Sophocles, can we assume that all members of a society may be satisfied this way? This provides us with a serious worry: can we do without work, or, rather, can we transform the nature of work in developed societies? Consider the all-too-credible description of the unemployed men in the bar in *Player Piano* – or, for that matter, the agreement across all political groups that our present high level of unemployment is unacceptable. We live in a society that views unemployment as a social ill. A social philosophy that causes an increased rate of formal unemployment – however creatively occupied this unemployment might be – presents certain problems.

Now these are problems that will have to be faced eventually: the sort of technological unemployment described in *Player Piano* will be ultimately unavoidable. But we do have a breathing space, since automation has not proceeded at the pace expected by many writers, and it may be possible to maintain 'full' employment in the current sense for perhaps another generation. We may, during that time, develop some methods for doing without jobs which are more palatable than those in Vonnegut's dystopia. But the trends we shall be discussing in this book seem to point in the direction of the dystopia, and not towards the much more attractive and gentle civilisation desired by Huxley, and by our four improvement theorists.

3 A Social Limit to Growth?

The foregoing discussion relies on the assumption that economic growth is possible. At the beginning of this decade such an assumption would have been a matter of controversy; various authorities, most notably the authors of the First Report of the Club of Rome,[5] put forward a neo-Malthusian view of continued economic growth surpassing the world's carrying capacity, leading to a global collapse. Such views are now unfashionable; many writers have argued convincingly that physical limits may be avoided by an appropriate combination of technical innovation and social reorganisation.[6] Recently however the debate has been reanimated. *Social Limits to Growth* by Fred Hirsch argues that the ultimate limit on economic growth is not physical, but is rather a result of the social nature of consumption. He states:

> Where the social environment has a restricted capacity for extending use without quality deterioration, it imposes social limits to consumption. More specifically, the limit is imposed on satisfactions that depend not on the product or facility in isolation but on the surrounding conditions of use. (Hirsch, *Social Limits to Growth*, p. 3)

The central concept in Hirsch's argument is social scarcity. He identifies two different cases. The first is of the class of goods which are not intrinsically desirable for any reason other than the fact of their scarcity; clearly, he claims, the supply of such goods cannot be increased by economic growth. The second is the class of goods which have some intrinsic value not directly dependent on their scarcity, but whose inherent desirability is nevertheless reduced by an extension in supply because of the resultant overcrowding. Leisure land is inherently desirable while it is isolated from noise and other people; when it is subdivided so as to be accessible to others its inherent amenity is reduced, since it is no longer isolated. It is not simply that the slices get smaller. A more familiar example is quoted by Hirsch on motoring: a pleasure while the number of cars is limited, but a pleasure that decreases progressively as the roads are filled. Similarly, increase in the supply of desirable social roles is restricted by an analogous process of 'social congestion'. Leadership positions are desirable both because of the freedom of action that leaders have, and because of the deference paid to them. If we increase the number of leadership positions, Hirsch argues, the inherent desirability of these roles is reduced. We cannot all stand on each other's shoulders.

Hirsch's argument is simply that, once past a certain level of subsistence, all the good things that society has to offer are positional. In seeking a real improvement in the quality of our lives we are running after our own shadows; any gain that we make is also made by those who were previously better-off than us, and who are therefore still better-off than us. And worse: this aimless pursuit has the effect of congesting the physical and social environment so that the good things we aspire to are less good than hitherto. Why then do we still want economic growth? Hirsch explains this as being a result of a divergence between individual and social rationality. Though as analysts standing outside society we may understand the implications of congestion, nevertheless as individual members of society we may still be tempted to ask: What difference will my car, my lakeside chalet, make to the congestion of the millions? Each individual is of course *individually* correct that his own effect is negligible, but when a million individuals make the same judgement simultaneously their effect is not negligible.

This is in essence a Malthusian position. It suggests that the demands of the many must necessarily outstrip any possible extension of the privileges of the few – a social Malthusianism to replace the now-unfashionable physical version. And the same objection can be brought to the social Malthusianism as to the physical. Limits on the supply of goods are merely apparent; with a little ingenuity we can often devise organisational or technical procedures to circumvent hindrances to growth.

Take, for example, Hirsch's first case, of 'pure' social scarcity. That a class of need whose 'satisfaction derives from scarcity itself' (p. 21) is subject to supply constraints is simply a tautology: objects that are valuable just because they are scarce cannot be plentiful. We have difficulty, however, in finding real objects which fall into this category. No-one, to the author's knowledge, collects Victorian farm workers' trouser buttons, even though they may be very scarce objects. Indeed, if people were to collect categories of uninteresting scarce objects, then the scarcity of the individual objects might well be so counterbalanced by the plenty of available categories for collection that the ownership of rarities would be open to all.

In real life, of course, objects which gain value because of their scarcity normally *also* have intrinsic worth. The ownership of original works of art, for example, gives two different sorts of benefit: from the direct experience of the work, and from the knowledge of the exclusive status ascribed to its owner. Now certainly, the supply of art objects is fixed at any point in time. The number of paintings by the masters of the past is finite (even though the definition of 'master' may change) and living artists have only a finite production. But nevertheless we may be able to increase the level of social benefit from fine art over time.

Economic growth might allow us to pay more artists to produce more works of art, and to buy old masterworks from private owners for public exhibition; the payments to the owners might be used to buy modern works.[7] Now consider the costs and benefits of such a growth in the stock of fine art objects. Certainly one of the two categories of pleasures of ownership – the exclusiveness – does become diluted. But this dilution does not affect the other category of benefit – pleasure in a work of art is not diminished by knowledge of others' similar pleasure; it may even be enhanced. And more people are getting this pleasure. So the growth in supply brings both costs and benefits: a diminution in the category of extrinsic benefits from exclusive ownership, and an increase in the intrinsic benefits arising from the experience of the work of art itself. We cannot calculate the net result without making some rather stringent assumptions about the justice of alternative distributions of the goods of society, but it is certainly clear that the result of the increase in the supply of works of art could be accounted as *pure* loss only by assuming that works of art have *no intrinsic value whatsoever*, which was probably not Hirsch's intention.

The general case seems to be that growth brings some costs because of 'congestion', and some benefits from wider access to good things, and that the balance may be tipped in the direction of the benefits by careful technical and organisational design. Take Hirsch's example of leisure land. He points out, quite correctly, that one weekend cottage by a lake gives a class of benefit that a village of such cottages clustering around the lake cannot; that we cannot, as a result of economic growth, all expect to have the lake to ourselves. Three sorts of qualification must be attached to this argument. First, weekend cottages are, by definition, not used at all for five-sevenths of the week, so that a simple organisational change could increase the effective supply by 250 per cent without significantly increasing congestion. Secondly, improvement in transport systems might bring more lakes within a suitable range for recreational use, and in the longer term, new forms of transport might make currently inaccessible areas such as mountain tops available for leisure purposes. Thirdly, even where an increase in supply does lead to losses from congestion, these losses, just as in the previous case of fine art, have to be set against the benefits accruing from wider access – though the owner of the once-isolated cottage loses his privacy, the visitors to the holiday village may be gaining leisure facilities where previously they had none.

Similar qualifications must be attached to Hirsch's other major example of congestion, the inherent scarcity of leadership roles in society. It is true that at any one time there are only a fixed number of leadership roles in a society, but the number may be increased over time. Particularly with economic growth it may be possible to reorganise social institutions in order to give more leadership roles, or to reduce the extent to which others are constrained by leaders. A case in point is the current interest in innovative forms of work organisation; experiments in participatory decision-making, industrial democracy and small-group production, seem to promise a general improvement in the nature of people's roles in the process of production.[8] Simply, small organisational units mean a large stock of leadership roles, and possibly more individual discretion for everyone. And the substance of leadership roles is not entirely debased by an increase in their numbers; though the esteem attached to them may be spread more thinly, this may be compensated for by the greater flexibility, the wider range of discretion enabled by a move from larger and inevitably more bureaucratic organisations to smaller scale organisations. Economic growth may in fact lead naturally to a beneficial increase in the number of leadership roles available.

Clearly, economic growth does not necessarily lead to congestion, since the stock of social goods may be increased. Congestion, as Hirsch describes it, is not a *limit* to growth but merely a *problem*. If we read his argument strictly as saying that economic growth has brought no benefits, that growth is merely a bidding-up of the price of scarce social goods, then we can test his position by looking at the consumption in the United Kingdom over the last twenty-five years to see if the real supply of goods has increased. Looking at the aggregate statistics it appears that the real disposable income of the average U.K. household rose by nearly 50 per cent over the last twenty-five years, that is, that people had the opportunity to consume many more social goods at the end of the period than they could at the beginning of it. Of course congestion must also have increased somewhat over this period. But any assertion such as Hirsch's that economic growth brings no real benefits makes the assumption that the increase in command over goods is insignificant when compared with the increase in congestion. This is in effect the same position as the liberal theorists' assumption of the satiation of the developed economies with material consumption. Chapter 5 will demonstrate that the empirical evidence of consumption patterns in the United Kingdom does not support this position.

Higher productivity and wider distribution of material goods is what growth is all about. Certainly, to the rich, this growth in material productivity means a double loss: they can no longer afford servants, and they must themselves work to provide their own services. And certainly the poor cannot expect, as a result of growth, to employ servants; but they can expect to enjoy services which they could not have done previously. The rich lose and the poor gain. A judgement of whether growth is a bad or a good thing depends on which side of the divide you stand. Hirsch's position is coherent; it is natural that the well-fed should wish to leave some eggs unbroken, but equally the hungry will want their omelettes. Hirsch's book hides judgements about the *desirability* of growth under apparently objectively-based pessimism about its *possibility*. He succeeds in demonstrating that some of the erstwhile privileges of the rich are not distributable, and that the poor are deluded if they think that they can succeed to those privileges as a result of growth. He does not succeed in showing that growth is impossible–but only that it brings some costs to the rich.

CHAPTER FOUR

TOWARDS A SERVICE ECONOMY?

1 What are Services?

Bell writes:

> . . . if an industrial society is defined by the quantity of goods as marking a standard of living, the post-industrial society is marked by the quality of life as measured by the services and amenities – health, education, recreation and the arts – which are now deemed desirable and possible for everyone. The word 'services' disguises different things and in the transformation of industrial to post-industrial society there are several different stages. First . . . a necessary expansion of transportation and public utilities as auxiliary service in the movement of goods. . . . Second, in the mass consumption of goods and the growth of population, there is an increase of distribution, finance, real estate and insurance, the traditional centres of white collar employment. Third, as national incomes rise as in the theorem of Christian Engel . . . the proportion of money devoted to food at home begins to drop, and marginal increments are used first for durables and then for luxury items, recreation and the like. Thus a third sector, that of personal services, begins to grow; restaurants, hotels, auto-services, travel, entertainments, sports, as people's horizons expand and new wants and tastes develop . . . two areas that are fundamental to [the good life] – health and education. (Bell, *The Coming of Post-Industrial Society*, pp. 127–8)

This is the central notion of the service economy in Bell's formulation. As economies 'modernise' and human labour becomes more productive, new demands are generated and the structure of the labour force changes so as to provide for these new demands. As Bell points out, this is the vision implicit in 'Engel's Law' of diminishing marginal expenditure on food with rising income – a vision of an established hierarchy of needs, such that as the more basic needs are progressively satisfied by the increasingly productive working population, so new needs arise, and the labour now unnecessary for the production of (relative) necessities is transferred to that of (relative) luxuries. As we gradually have our fill of material goods, so our aspirations turn to the consumption of immaterial services. This is Bell's explanation of the service economy; 'From Goods to Services', as his chapter title has it, the service worker comes to predominate because of unsatisfied social demands for the consumption of non-material products.

Despite this, Bell never directly tells us what a 'service' is; he defines 'service workers' by inclusion, as in such passages as the one quoted above, but he never explicitly describes this attribute of 'service' that they have in common. Of course, it becomes obvious by contrast with the nature of 'goods'; goods are material, permanent, made by people using machines, which are sold or otherwise distributed to people who thereafter may use them at their will. Services, we infer by contrast, are immaterial, impermanent, made by people for people ('post-industrial society is essentially a game between persons') and consumable only at the instant of production. At the moment of its acquisition by the consumer, a good is a *thing* whereas a service is a *state* or *activity* or *sensation*. Why is it necessary to qualify this statement by confining it to the moment of acquisition? Simply, because even goods eventually supply a service. Or, to put it another way, both goods and services answer needs, and generally the same needs may be met by either goods or services. If I want my back scratched, I can either hire the services of a service worker, the back-scratcher, who will ply his trade for so much an hour, or else invest in a good, an electric back-scratcher, which I may acquire over the counter for so much down, and which I may use thereafter at my whim. The satisfaction I derive from each course of action is potentially identical, and if I am in a rational mood I choose between them on the grounds of cost. Services are distinct from goods only as alternative means, alternative social arrangements, for meeting needs.

What Bell is asking us to believe, at its simplest, is that the new needs that emerge as societies get richer are in some way necessarily more demanding of personal services for their satisfaction. As times change, new technologies develop, new social arrangements arise, and old needs are met in new ways. Bell's thesis requires that of necessity the balance of provision for needs over time is increasingly by service rather than by goods, but he provides no evidence to demonstrate that this has been so in the past. Although he adopts growth in the final consumption of services as his explanation for the growth in the number of service workers, he only gives us data on his *explicand*, the size of the service employment sector. The following discussion suggests that in some cases – in the United Kingdom and by presumption in other developed countries – the consumption of services has actually fallen, precisely because of changes in technology and social arrangements. It points out that the overall rise in consumption of services is both unnecessary and insufficient to explain the rise of the service employment sector, and suggests that we have no reason to suppose the inevitability of future increases in the consumption of services. For the moment, however, we shall consider only the *unnecessary* nature of Bell's explanation of the growth of the service sector. We can propose (and will later substantiate) a number of alternative explanations.

The most interesting of these explanations rests on an alternative definition of the service sector, a definition which we can draw from an often misapplied passage from the *Wealth of Nations*:

> [The work of servants] . . . consists in services which perish generally in the very instant of their performance, and does not fix or realise itself in any vendible commodity which can replace the value of their wages and maintenance. The labour, on the contrary, of artificers, manufacturers and merchants, naturally does fix and realise itself in some such commodity. (Smith, *The Wealth of Nations*, Bk IV, ch. IX)[1]

Many writers classify service occupations as Adam Smith does domestic servants; 'I have classed [them] . . . among the barren or unproductive'. Bell largely accepts this evaluation, arguing, however, that we must use other than merely economic criteria in their assessment – indeed, it is precisely this impossibility to account adequately for the benefits from services in material terms that leads him to argue for the coming necessity for 'social' rather than 'economic' accounting. But Adam Smith is himself careful to stress that merchants – clearly a service occupation – are to be classed among the productive. Why he should choose to exclude domestic functions from the division of labour, and place servants outside the chain of production, is a subject for speculation – sexism? absent-mindedness? – but whatever the reason, we can only consider it arbitrary and misleading.

What differs between service and other occupations is not their productivity – for who can say that the design engineer, or the draughtsman, is any more or less productive than the turner in the tool room – but rather their closeness to the physical transformation of material. The difference between the valet and the merchant, like that between the merchant and the shop-floor worker, is merely one of degree – he is several links in the chain of production further away from the material production of goods. This alternative definition of 'service workers', relative distance from material production, has nothing to do with the nature of the final product (for Bell, as we said above, the service worker makes services) but rather with the nature of his job. Service workers by this definition may produce bicycles or machine tools just as well as education or entertainment. Bell implicitly accepts this second definition, for he includes engineers, for example, as members of the coming dominant service class, but nevertheless, he cannot have taken it fully on board, for it would surely have suggested to him an alternative explanation for the growth in the service sector; that service jobs, in this second sense, are instrumental to the increase of material production.

Is it not possible that we have more engineers because our methods of production have become more complex? That our universities expand because we need more engineers? Let us be clear here; the two questions imply that we can explain the growth of a service sector, the university, by new demand for material production from manufacturing industry. This is not to say that the growth of the university was a necessary consequence of the demands of manufacturing industry. This higher productivity could have been achieved by an expansion of production in the computer industry in the form of teaching machines for the automatic programmed instruction of more engineers. Certainly, a higher 'final' demand for education as a good-in-itself might be sufficient for growth in the education service sector, but that demand is not a necessary cause, nor is the growth a necessary result.

So we have identified a fallacy. Once we realise that service occupations may just as well be engaged in the production of goods as of services, and that needs we customarily consider as calling for services might as well be met by goods, we must also understand that the identity that Bell asserts between the growth in service employment and the growth in demand for services is a false one. In this chapter and the two which follow, we shall examine the two elements of this identity to get some idea of what sorts of changes are taking place in the distribution of occupation and the pattern of consumption.

2 Growing Service Employment

We must start by making an important distinction between two different types of employment classification. The first is employment as classified by industrial sector, so that no matter what the nature of the particular job, be it manual, clerical, technical or administrative, it appears under the title of its eventual product. The industrial classification of coal mining thus includes doctors, lawyers and accountants. The occupational classification, on the other hand, looks only to the nature of the job, and not to the product, so that when we look later at the cross-tabulation of occupations across industries, we will see these same doctors, lawyers and accountants classed in professional occupations even though their industrial classification is as coal mining workers.

At first glance, these two classifications might appear to coincide with the two alternative ways of distinguishing between goods and services described in the previous section; that the industrial classification would indicate the relative proportions of goods and services consumed by the society, whereas the occupational classification indicates the proportion of service to other jobs. This is in fact not so. While the equivalence holds for the 'occupational' classification, it does not do so for the product classification. By 'consumed by society' we refer to 'final consumption', the use of products by consumers as an end in itself, and not by other producers as a means of further production. The use by the Coal Board of the professional services of those lawyers and accountants is in this sense 'intermediate consumption', whereas the services on behalf of private individuals is 'final'. The size of any particular industrial sector does not indicate the size of its final product; the machine tool industry, for example, though of critical importance for the economy as a whole, has only a tiny final output in comparison to its intermediate product. A growth of the service sector in the industrial classification might, in the absence of any other information, indicate a change in the organisation of manufacturing industry so that fewer professional workers are full-time employees, and more are acting as self-employed consultants with no increase in final demand for services. This is not itself an explanation that should be advanced at this point in the argument, though later we shall consider examples of equivalent expansion in apparently 'service' industries, but it does demonstrate the possibility of such a growth without any equivalent increase in the final consumption of services. In this chapter we shall in fact use the industrial classification only as an inferior surrogate for the occupational one which, though better for our purpose, is less easily available for some countries.

We can start by considering the U.K. occupational distribution, and its change since the middle of the last century, when the population census first collected the information – see Table 4.1.[2] This is not a very reliable data set; the categories and the criteria for inclusion have varied greatly over the period, and before 1951 the industrial classification is only inferred from

TABLE 4.1   *Percentage distribution among industries of the working population in the United Kingdom, 1841–1971*

	1841	1861	1881	1901	1921	1951	1971
Primary							
Agriculture and mining	25.5	23.2	17.9	14.8	14.4	8.9	4.4
Secondary							
Manufacturing	35.5	38.6	36.5	37.9	36.2	39.0	34.9
Intermediate							
Transport, communication, utilities, construction	8.4	11.3	13.7	16.3	12.2	14.0	15.4
Tertiary							
Services, white collar	23.1*	21.2	24.5	25.1	35.1	37.7	45.3
Other	7.5	5.6	7.3	5.9	2.2	0.4	–

* Including approximately 4 per cent coachmen, grooms, etc.

occupations (we shall return to this distinction in the next chapter). But, such as it is, it does provide us with the opportunity of considering some quite definite long-term trends.

The two trends which show up most clearly concern the primary industries and services. The primary industries are declining; with one exception, the percentage of the working population employed in the primary sector has fallen every decade since, at the latest, 1841. But even this simple statistic disguises two contrary trends; though agriculture has fallen monotonically through this period, employment in mining rose continuously through the first half, a fact which appears only fleetingly in the aggregate primary sector statistics as a small increase between 1891 and 1901 – see Table 4.2. Similarly, the

TABLE 4.2 *Percentages in agriculture and mining in the United Kingdom, 1841–1971*

	1841	1861	1881	1901	1921	1951	1971
Agriculture	22.2	18.8	13.1	9.0	7.9	5.9	3.6
Mining	3.3	4.4	4.8	5.8	6.5	3.0	1.0

steady rise of service employment over this period (the fall between 1841 and 1851 merely betokens the transfer of grooms and coachmen into the 'intermediate' category) hides a number of quite contrary trends. To take the most obvious of these, while, as in Table 4.3, the white collar category has risen continuously throughout this period, the proportion of other services initially rises, and only falls to its present low level comparatively late in the period.

The most important point to emerge from this is that the more we disaggregate these statistics, the less tidy the patterns become. This applies to each of the sectors. Though the proportion in

TABLE 4.3 *Percentages in white-collar and domestic employment in the United Kingdom, 1841–1971*

	1841	1861	1881	1901	1921	1951	1971
White collar	4.4	4.9	7.4	9.7	24.7	30.3	39.6
Other services	14.7*	16.3	17.1	15.4	10.4	7.4	5.7

* Excluding an estimated 4 per cent for coachmen, grooms, etc.

manufacturing industry has, with the exception of the depression years of the early 1930s, stayed within 3 per cent of its 1841 value, still whole industries have successively boomed and fallen into decay. In the 'intermediate' category, the growth in numbers of construction workers is compounded with the twentieth-century decline in number of railway and public utility workers. While our observations of the occupational pattern are more-or-less consistent with Bell's description, we must add a caution; growth in service categories has a different nature at different points in time. Between 1841 and 1901, increase in service employment meant predominantly increasing numbers of female domestic servants; between 1981 and 1991 it will mean . . . more social workers? . . . more astrophysicists?

We must take care how we think about these long-term changes; we must avoid the temptation to think of them as growth in one sector at the expense of some other. Robert Heilbronner has recently argued that since the proportion of the total workforce in manufacturing industry in the United States has fallen by less than 5 per cent since 1900, and the fall of the proportion in agriculture (from 38 per cent to 4 per cent) is approximately balanced by the rise in services (from 24 per cent to 64 per cent), one *explains* the other, that in some sense declining agricultural employment has pushed workers into services, or that booming services have pulled workers from agriculture.[3] This is not a very satisfactory argument. First of all, it commits a fallacy of aggregation; even if these changes were to take place over a short period of time, we could still not assume that the flow of the labour force was directly from agriculture to services – it might well have been from agriculture into a booming section of manufacturing industry, and from a slumping section of manufacturing industry into services. Second, it ignores the turnover in membership of the workforce; seventy years is one-and-a-half working lives, and to make any attribution of a direct transition over such a period would involve, to say the least, a dubious assumption about social mobility. And finally, the absolute size of the U.S. workforce has grown somewhat over the period (from 29 million to 50 million), so that though the proportions balance, the total numbers changing occupation certainly do not.

Though Heilbronner's proposition is not really convincing, the pattern of thought that it exemplifies is still seductive. We are all too likely to think of changes in occupational distribution in terms of smooth transitions coinciding with the stages of economic growth; agricultural workers moving to industry, industrial workers to transport and the utilities, utilities to personal services. The reality is, however, much less tidy. We can get some idea of the actual occupational transitions which take place from information contained in the 1971 United Kingdom Population Census which plots occupation changes between 1970 and 1971. If we consider the 27 'Minimum List' occupational classifications (excluding new entry and retirement), we find that during this year 13.9 per cent of the working population changed their occupation. (If we considered changing occupations within these categories the total would be approximately 40 per cent.) Aggregating further into Bell's occupational sectors, we can construct the transition matrix in Table 4.4. In this matrix, the content of each cell is the percentage of the total

TABLE 4.4 *Transition between occupational sectors in the United Kingdom, 1970–71, in percentage of total workforce*

		Occupations in 1970				
		Farms and mines	Blue collar	Personal services	Other white collar	
Occupations in 1971	Farms and mines	3.11	0.05	0.01	0.02	3.19
	Blue collar	0.09	44.58	0.21	0.50	45.38
	Personal services	0.01	0.27	11.20	0.23	11.71
	Other white collar	0.02	0.56	0.23	38.91	39.72

workforce in both the horizontal category in 1970 and the vertical category in 1971. The top-left-to-bottom-right diagonal contains those who have not changed their occupation during this period; the sum of this diagonal is 97.8, so that 2.2 per cent of the working population has changed occupational sector. But we notice that the changes are in all directions, that each cell has some content and, further, that changes often cancel out – for example, 0.2 per cent changed from farm to white collar occupations, and similarly, 0.2 per cent from white collar to farming, so that the net movements are very much smaller (see Table 4.5). The changes are all as we would expect, from farming to manufacturing, from manufacturing to services and white collar occupations, but they are tiny even in relation to all movements across occupational sector boundaries (which are 13.75 times more frequent), let alone in relation to those between minimum list categories, which are many times more frequent than movements across sector boundaries. So we must view individuals in occupational transition almost like molecules in Brownian motion, a flurry of frantic activity which amounts to only the smallest of net change.

TABLE 4.5 *Net transition between occupations in the United Kingdom, 1970–71, in percentage of total workforce*

		Farms and mines	Blue collar	Personal services	Other white collar
Occupations in 1971	Farms and mines	–			
	Blue collar	0.04	–		
	Personal services	0.00	0.06	–	
	Other white collar	0.00	0.06	0.00	–

Occupations in 1970

Of course, we cannot generalise very far from these observations of one year in the United Kingdom: it was a year of economic depression, and one year is a very short period in relation to the time scales we are describing, so the actual numbers involved may be misleading. Yet, interpreted loosely, its implications may be more broadly applicable. We have no reason to suppose that the changes in totals employed in each occupational category represent all or even the major changes in the economy. Indeed, to the extent that we can generalise from the United Kingdom 1970–71 data, such changes in occupational distribution due to long-term patterns of social and technical change are quite insignificant in comparison with the process of exchanging occupations for personal reasons. Occupational transition resulting from structural change is merely the residual of the (much larger) total occupational flux.

If we consider the historical growth of employment sectors in

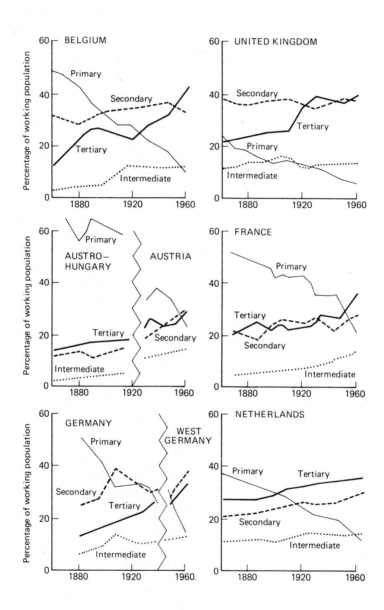

FIGURE 4.1 *Sectoral employment distributions in six European states, 1860–1960*

European countries, we can identify a complex pattern of development – see Figure 4.1. We can see that the proportion employed in agriculture declines over time; that employment in manufacturing industry increases initially, levels off and finally declines; that after initial fluctuations, the proportion of service employment rises over time. Of these, over this period, only agriculture represents a clear trend – all the rest are simply tendencies, with numerous divergences.

As we come to the present day, we see these trends and tendencies much more strongly confirmed. In all O.E.C.D. countries since 1960, the employment proportion in primary industries has fallen; in all but two (and in these two cases the data may be at fault) the proportion in tertiary industry has risen. Table 4.6 summarises the pattern of change. Eight out of the nine countries in category 1 (the exception being Luxembourg) might be classed as 'less developed' within the O.E.C.D., whereas the thirteen in category 2 would all be considered 'more developed'. The pattern of change we are observing is certainly systematic. This emerges much more clearly by correlating these two categories with G.D.P. per head in the O.E.C.D. countries – see

TABLE 4.6[4] *Change in sectoral employment patterns in O.E.C.D. states, 1960–74*

1 Primary decreasing, secondary, intermediate and tertiary increasing	2 Primary decreasing, secondary and/or inter- mediate decreasing, tertiary increasing	3 Other
Portugal Spain Turkey Ireland Luxembourg Greece Japan Austria Italy	Sweden Switzerland Netherlands Norway Belgium Denmark Finland France Germany Canada United States New Zealand United Kingdom	Iceland Australia
Total in category 9	13	2

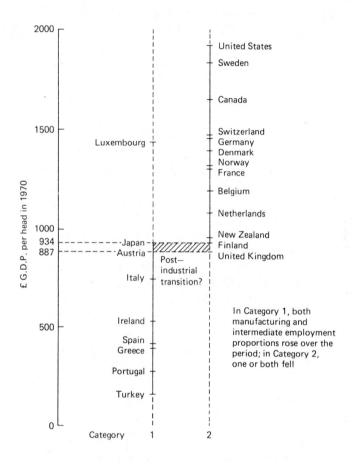

FIGURE 4.2 *Employment changes and gross domestic product in the O.E.C.D., 1960–74*

Figure 4.2. As it stands, this seems to constitute quite a powerful developmental model.[5]

These same trends are seen when we consider the more detailed pattern of recent change in industrial employment in Great Britain – see Table 4.7.

Before continuing, we should introduce a note of caution. There are two main sources for employment statistics in the United Kingdom; the Population Census and information drawn from National Insurance returns. The Census, though reason-

TABLE 4.7   *Industrial employment in Great Britain, 1948–76, as percentage of workforce*

	1948	1951	1956	1961	1966	1971	1976
Primary	8.5	7.8	7.0	5.8	4.5	3.4	3.2
Secondary	39.7	41.6	42.2	39.3	38.5	37.9	32.8
Intermediate	16.8	16.4	16.1	15.7	15.7	14.7	13.6
(Transport and							
communication)	(8.7)	(8.3)	(7.9)	(7.4)	(6.9)	(7.1)	(6.5)
Tertiary	34.5	34.0	34.6	38.7	41.3	43.4	50.4

ably reliable, suffers as a source for our purposes from its infrequency; for more data over a shorter period of time we have to rely on the National Insurance returns, even though they are systematically warped by avoidance of National Insurance payments. This biases estimates of the 'intermediate' category and also of service workers. An alternative estimate of the number of service workers, drawn from the Census, is shown in Table 4.8. The direction of the trends is, however, apparently not affected. Even making this correction, we see a very large movement towards service sector employment, and a similar one

TABLE 4.8   *Tertiary employment as a percentage of the workforce*

	1951	1961	1966	1971
Tertiary percentage	37.7	40.4	42.7	45.3

away from manufacturing industry. While this corresponds to the trends identified by Bell, the behaviour of the intermediate category does not. We see employment in transport declining, directly contradicting the prediction quoted at the beginning of this chapter – or does it? Bell in fact merely predicts an 'expansion of transportation and public utilities as auxiliary service in the movement of goods' – that there is more need for transport, and not that the number of those employed in providing transport as a service would increase. And, of course, the falling number of 'transport employees' merely reflects an increasing tendency for both private individuals and firms to consume transport in the form of a good instead of a service – to *buy* cars and lorries instead of *using* trains or buses – and while the staff of declining public transport systems appear in the 'intermediate' category, the workers in motor vehicle factories are to be found in the 'manufacturing' category. In fact, none of the occupational patterns we have observed here have any direct relevance to Bell's 'goods to services' prediction, since he is talking about *final* consumption, which has no necessary connection with employment patterns.

3 Service Employment and the Service Economy

In this chapter we have shown a convincing pattern of growth of service employment in both the United Kingdom and the developed world, a pattern which may be traced back at least to the middle of the last century. As regards the United Kingdom at least, we have argued that this growth cannot be explained by the decline of primary employment. And we have observed a highly determined pattern of change among the sectors between 1960 and 1974 for almost all O.E.C.D. countries, such that employment in manufacturing or intermediate industry rose among the less-developed states and fell among the more developed. Nevertheless, this striking pattern of development, when correctly viewed, does not provide evidence supporting Bell's service economy thesis.

It fails to do so because of two serious errors in the logic of the service economy thesis. The thesis has, in essence, three stages: first, as we get richer, we develop new categories of needs or demands; second, these new needs have to be met by services rather than by goods; third, an increase in the demand for services leads to increased numbers in service employment. Bell provides us only with data to substantiate the final prediction of increased service employment, which we have shown in this chapter to be an accurate generalisation for the whole of the developed world. But, as we have suggested, to take this generalisation as evidence for the whole 'goods to services' thesis involves an invalidly reversed implication; for while increased service consumption necessarily requires more service workers, more service workers do not necessarily imply more consumption of services, for *service workers are also concerned in the manufacture of goods*. So we have an alternative model to present; in Chapter 5 we shall show that while new categories of demand have come with increasing wealth, they have been satisfied more by goods than by services; and in Chapter 6 we shall investigate the number of tertiary workers who are actually involved in the production of goods.

CHAPTER FIVE

THE SELF-SERVICE ECONOMY

1 The Consumption of Services

At the centre of the service economy argument is 'Engel's Law', which says that we have a hierarchy of needs, and that as the most pressing are satisfied, so our increasing means are devoted to the less pressing; that is, that our proportionate marginal expenditure on necessities decreases as our income increases. We can most easily visualise this theorem in the form shown in Figure 5.1. The expenditure categories a, b and c are ranked according to their significance – a meets the most pressing needs, c the least. We see on the diagram that as the size of the weekly budget increases, the proportion of it spent on a decreases, on b, first increases and then decreases, and on c continuously increases. We might alternatively represent expenditure on each category as a proportion of the total; in which case we get Figure 5.2.

Engel's original formulation was based on his empirical observation of the decreasing proportion of expenditure on food. Bell, as we see from the quotation on p. 55, would similarly classify food as a category of expenditure which behaves as a in

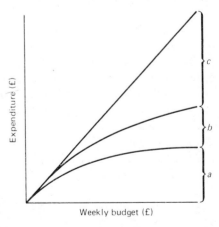

FIGURE 5.1 *'Engel's Law'*

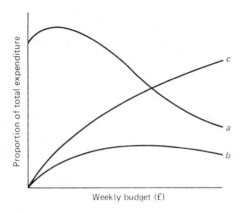

FIGURE 5.2   *Engel's Law: proportions of expenditure*

our diagram, and further specifies that consumption of durable goods behaves as *b*, and consumption of services grows as *c*. Does this really happen? We can see if it does in the United Kingdom by examining the data from the Household Expenditure Survey presented in Figure 5.3. If we express these categories of expenditure as a proportion of the budget in each year, we derive Table 5.1. Proportional expenditure on food has indeed decreased through the twenty-year period – but expenditure on services has stayed constant. The largest proportionate rise by far is that of transport, and transport is indeed mentioned by Bell as one of the services he expects to increase. But is transport a service product according to our definition? Certainly, some sorts of transport are: public transport is an 'activity' rather than a 'thing', and requires the cooperation of service workers, but a motor car is equally a 'thing' and requires no such cooperation. If we disaggregate the 'transport' expenditure category into its 'goods related' and 'service related' parts, we see (Table 5.2) that all the growth relates to the motor car, and that the 'service' provisions of transport – railways, buses and other public transport – have actually declined as a proportion of expenditure.

So as far as household expenditure in the United Kingdom goes, we cannot see the post-industrial growth in the consumption of services. Households in 1974, though they are nearly

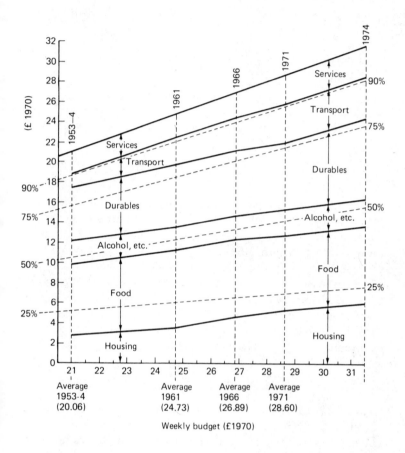

FIGURE 5.3 *Changing expenditure patterns of the average household, 1953–74*

TABLE 5.1 *Percentage of household expenditure in the United Kingdom, 1954–74*

	1954	1961	1966	1971	1974
House and heating	14.1	15.4	17.5	18.8	19.0
Food	33.4	30.4	28.2	25.9	24.5
Alcohol and tobacco	10.2	9.5	9.4	8.9	8.4
Durables and clothing	25.8	24.5	23.8	23.0	24.6
Transport	7.1	10.3	11.8	13.7	13.4
Services	9.5	9.5	9.4	9.4	9.6

TABLE 5.2 *Substitution of transport goods for services in the United Kingdom, 1954–74*

		1954	1961	1966	1971	1974
As percentage of total expenditure	Transport goods	3.5	7.2	8.6	10.8	11.1
	Transport services	3.5	3.1	3.2	2.9	2.4
As percentage of transport expenditure	Transport goods	50.0	69.9	72.9	78.8	82.2
	Transport services	50.0	30.1	27.1	21.1	17.8

50 per cent richer in real terms than in 1954, still spend the same proportion of their budget on the items in this category, on cinemas, theatres, sport and entertainment, licensing and renting radio and television, domestic help, laundry, payments to charities–all the things that, following Bell, we should have expected to be rising faster than the other categories of expenditure. (Medical and educational facilities in the United Kingdom are, of course, largely provided by the state, and we will consider them separately.) So we are left with a question; why does the extension of Engel's Law not hold?

2 Substitution of Goods for Services

Central to the appeal of this Engel's Law is its intuitive correlation with the results of our own introspection. We all know, when we think about it, that if we were a little richer *at this moment*, we would spend our money differently – certainly we would maintain the roof over our heads, and the supply of breakfast cereal, but equally, we might spend a new increment of income, not on more food, but on, say, opera tickets. And indeed, we can obtain empirical answers to this question, applicable to a whole population, by discovering the pattern of expenditure, at one point in time, of numbers of individuals (or, since they are the main spending unit, households) with different budgets. When we take such a cross-sectional 'snapshot' of spending patterns, we do find the patterns predicted by the static version of Engel's Law – see Figure 5.4. In 1954 we find the proportional expenditure on food decreasing continuously with size of household

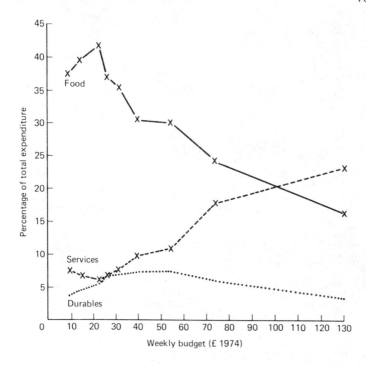

FIGURE 5.4 *Household expenditure on three consumption categories in the United Kingdom, 1954*

budget, except for the very poorest of the poor for whom other necessities (housing and clothing), briefly take priority. We find the proportional expenditure on durables rising initially and subsequently falling, and we see the proportion spent on services rising continuously with wealth. Furthermore, we might surmise that proportional service expenditure in the richest group was generally higher than appears here, since the data is influenced unduly by one single case. To quote the indignant footnote appended to the entry for this group in the 'women's outer clothing category': 'One member of a household in this group spent £1903 on one item during the period when records were being kept'! So, in this 'cross-sectional' interpretation, Engel's Law seems to hold; why can we not therefore apply it across time? The answer becomes apparent as soon as we compare two

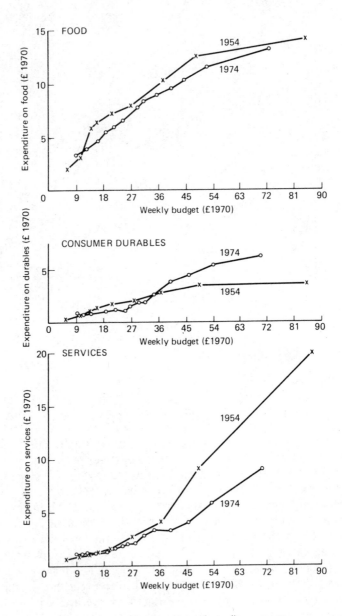

FIGURE 5·5   *Changing patterns of expenditure, 1954–74*

of these 'cross-sectional' pictures for different points in time – see Figure 5.5.

The answer is that the curves have shifted over time; the 1974 expenditure distributions still show the same 'cross-sectional' Engel's Law configuration, with falling food and durables proportions and (generally) rising consumption of services. But the 1974 service curve lies, in real terms, below the 1954 one, because for any budgetary level, the marginal propensity to consume services (the proportion of each extra £1 spent on services) is lower in 1974 than in 1954, so that although the country may have got richer, the proportion spent on services stays reasonably constant. Similarly, the proportion spent on food decreases, and that on durables increases. It is tempting to try to explain these shifts of expenditure cross-sections over time; we might, for example, try to demonstrate their independence of price changes by considering the income elasticities of demand – the effect on the relative desirabilities of the goods of a change in the size of the household's budget – or else enter a Galbraith-type argument about the proliferation of demand for flippant consumer items due to advertising pressures. But, for the purposes of this argument, we do not need to attribute a cause to these changes, but merely to observe their occurrence. We can see the pattern of change by considering the proportion of service expenditure on individual items in Table 5.3. We see the steep drop in expenditure on entertainment outside the home, the rise in the proportionate expenditure on renting and licensing

TABLE 5.3   *Summary of service expenditure in the United Kingdom, as percentage of total budget, 1954–74*

	1954	1961	1966	1971	1974
Transport services	3.5	3.1	3.2	2.9	2.4
Post and telecommunications	0.6	0.7	0.8	1.0	1.1
Cinemas and theatres	2.0	1.0	1.0	0.8	0.8
Domestic help and laundry	1.6	1.2	1.1	0.8	0.8
Hairdressing, repairs	1.2	1.4	1.2	0.9	0.9
Television licence and rent	0.3	1.0	1.2	1.2	1.4
Medical and education	1.0	1.0	0.7	0.8	0.9
Holidays, etc.	2.9	3.1	3.3	3.7	3.8
All services (including transport services, excluding purchase and running of motor cars)	13.1	12.5	12.5	12.1	12.1

televisions, the decline in domestic help, the increase in expenditure on holiday travel. Those items in the list with most person-to-person contact show reductions, those mediated by machine increase. We can perhaps throw some light on these changes by juxtaposing a number of aggregated categories, as in Table 5.4. We see domestic service being replaced by domestic machines; we see personal entertainment 'services' (by our definition of transient state or activity) replaced by entertainment goods, transport services by transport goods.

TABLE 5.4 *Some selected expenditure categories as percentage of total United Kingdom budget, 1954–74*

	1954	1961	1966	1971	1974
Cinemas, theatres, etc.	2.0	1.0	1.0	0.6	0.8
Television: buy and rent	1.4	2.1	2.1	2.3	3.0
Domestic help and laundry	1.6	1.2	1.1	0.8	0.8
Domestic appliances	0.8	1.7	1.4	1.5	1.7
Transport services	3.5	3.1	3.2	2.9	2.4
Transport goods	3.5	7.2	8.6	10.8	11.1

		1954	1974			1954	1974
Percentage of budget	Selected services	7.1	4.0	Percentage of total in these categories	Selected services	55.5	20.2
	Selected goods	5.7	15.8		Selected goods	44.5	79.8
		12.8	19.8			100.0	100.0

We can go further. So far we have considered merely the proportion of the total budget being spent on these various categories. Where we have wanted to compare expenditures at different dates, we have merely inflated expenditures by the aggregate consumer price index. But this does not give us a very good indication of the quantities of the various goods and services that are being consumed, since subsumed within the aggregate price index are numbers of different price trends for different commodities. Prices of all goods and services do not rise at equal rates; in particular, prices of services rose between 1954 and 1974 considerably faster than those of durable goods. If we set the aggregate price index to 100 in 1954, it stands at 267.8 in 1974; in comparison, the consumer durable index has only risen to 187.0 over that period, whereas the price of services has risen to 321.5. The price of services throughout the period was rising 1.72 times as fast as that of durables. This means that if we want to get some indication of the relative real consumption of these commodities, as opposed to the budgetary proportion they represent, we should deflate each category by its particular price index, rather than the aggregate one, as shown in Figure 5.6. (We have to be careful to stress that this procedure only gives an indication of compara-

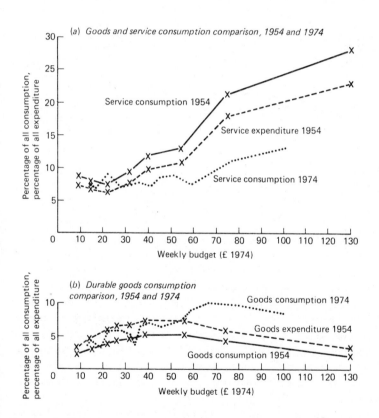

FIGURE 5.6 *Real consumption of durables and services in the United Kingdom, 1954 and 1974 ('Real consumption' estimated by inflating 1954 expenditure by the price index for the individual commodity; 'expenditure proportion' estimated by inflating 1954 expenditure with overall consumer price index.)*

tive real consumption – the nature of the actual commodities has changed over the period, so that it is possible that the price indices for different dates refer to different standards of value.)

When we deflate by this procedure, we can easily see that the trend towards increased real consumption of material goods is quite considerable, and that there has been a definite drop in the consumption of services. And if we similarly deflate our previous table relating reduction of 'service' items to the compensating increases in the equivalent goods, we see an even more marked pattern of substitution for services with equivalent goods – see Table 5.5.

TABLE 5.5   *Estimated real consumption of selected goods and services in the United Kingdom, 1954–74; inflating by price indices for individual categories*

		1954	1974		1954	1974
Services	Cinemas, theatres, etc., domestic help, laundry, transport services	8.5	4.0	As percentage of total in categories	69.7	20.2
Goods	Television (buying and renting), domestic appliances, motor cars	3.7	15.8		30.3	79.8
Total		12.2	19.8		100	100

In this section, we have seen that, excluding education and medicine, consumption to meet the sorts of needs which Daniel Bell identifies as characterising post-industrial society has risen, but that these newly-dominant needs are met, not by services, but by goods. We must, however, be careful about the use of the word 'consumption' here. When we consume services, the state or condition we pay for disappears after a short period; clothes cleaned by a laundry become dirty – and the service has been *literally* consumed, vanished away, not to return. But when we come into possession of a washing machine, we do not expect our purchase to vanish after first use – indeed, we buy it on the assumption that it will persist for some years. Were it not that the benefit from the domestic washing machine goes in kind entirely to the household that possesses it, so that its product is not accounted for in the national product, we would certainly consider the household's purchase, not as consumption, but as investment. This growth in consumption of goods represents a fundamental change in the nature of economic activity. Instead of capital investment taking place in industry, and industry providing services for individuals and households, increasingly, capital investment takes place in households, leaving industry engaged in what is essentially intermediate production, making the capital goods – the cookers, freezers, televisions, motor cars – used in home production of the final product. This is the trend towards the do-it-yourself economy – almost the antithesis of Bell's service economy. Now, certainly we have so far ignored the two areas of service consumption which have grown over the past two decades: medicine and education. Indeed, in the following section we shall observe that when we include these two areas, service expenditure as a whole has risen slightly. But, and this is the crux of our difference with Bell, why should we assume that consumption of these two items will necessarily continue to rise? Can we not see pressures for education and medicine to go the same way as other 'post industrial' household expenditure. Can we not imagine the replacement of social investment in educational and medical plant by household investment in educational and medical machines? We shall return to this supposition later.

3 Growing Social Expenditure on Services

So far we have considered only household expenditure; we have to consider in addition government expenditures. We find (Table 5.6) that there has been considerable growth in services. Over

TABLE 5.6 *Government expenditure on services in the United Kingdom, 1954–74, as percentage of total government expenditure*

	1954	1961	1966	1971	1974
Housing and environmental services	1.6	2.5	5.8	6.5	6.4
Libraries, museums, arts	–	0.7	0.8	0.9	1.0
Police, prisons, fire service, Parliament, Law Courts	3.0	4.9	5.4	6.6	6.7
Education	12.7	17.1	18.0	18.8	20.8
National Health Service	16.4	19.1	19.5	20.2	21.0
Personal social services	–	–	0.8	2.8	3.5

the period 1954–74, services rose from nearly 34 per cent of U.K. Public Authorities' current expenditure to nearly 60 per cent, with the vast bulk of expenditure on medical services and education, which are precisely the growth areas identified by Bell. So, to this extent only, our findings support Bell; he does correctly identify the actual areas of past growth in the U.K. public services.

However, when we tie the private and public expenditures together, we find that this growth is of only marginal significance: public current expenditure is still less than one-quarter of total current expenditure, so that though public expenditure on services dwarfs that of the private sector, both together are still less than one-third of private expenditure on goods. We can build up a clear picture of the overall relationship between goods and services from the National Accounts. To begin with, consider the three components of national expenditure – Table 5.7. Of these, we have already considered consumer expenditure; on the basis of household expenditure we estimated services to be around nine or ten per cent of the total throughout the period – the estimate here, with expenditure on food outside the home added, is slightly higher, falling from 11.9 per cent in 1954 to 10.6 per cent in 1974 – see Table 5.8. We have already considered (in Table 5.6) the

TABLE 5.7   *Domestic expenditure in the United Kingdom, 1954–74, in current £ million*

	1954	1961	1966	1971	1974
Consumers' expenditure	12091	17835	24246	35075	51670
Public authorities' current expenditure	3182	4584	6572	10353	16641
Capital formation and increase in stocks	2651	4983	7261	10477	17329
Total domestic expenditure	17924	27402	38079	55905	85640

TABLE 5.8   *Consumer expenditure in the United Kingdom, 1954–74, in current £ million*

	1954	1961	1966	1971	1974
Consumers' expenditures on service	1433	2056	2747	3693	5500
Consumers' expenditures on goods	10658	15779	21499	31382	46170

service elements in public authorities' current expenditure; the balance in absolute terms is shown in Table 5.9.

TABLE 5.9 *Public expenditure in the United Kingdom, 1954–74, in current £ million*

	1954	1961	1966	1971	1974
Public expenditure on services	1074	2027	3308	5873	9898
Public expenditure on goods	2108	2557	3264	4480	6743

It is, however, rather more difficult to disentangle the 'goods-related' from the 'service-related' elements in capital formation. The estimates we might make would not be very reliable, but it is clear that overall investment in the services is very low by comparison with that in goods-producing industries, so we shall restrict ourselves to estimating current expenditure.

Putting these tables together, we finally arrive at Table 5.10. The price of services to the household rose over this period 20 per cent faster than the average rise in prices. So, assuming a similar rise in the price of public services, 1974 real consumption of services in terms comparable with the 1954 estimate was only 19.6 per cent. This rise of 3.4 per cent in the service consumption proportion is not really very significant over a twenty-year period.

TABLE 5.10 *Services as percentage of United Kingdom consumption, 1954–74, in current £ million*

	1954	1961	1966	1971	1974
Service as percentage of consumer expenditure	11.85	11.53	11.33	10.53	10.64
Service as percentage of public expenditure	33.80	44.21	50.33	56.73	59.50
Service as percentage of all current expenditure	16.40	18.20	19.64	21.06	22.54

Certainly at 22.5 per cent of all current expenditure (and presumably at something less than 20 per cent of final domestic expenditure) services are an important part of the United Kingdom's economic activity. But is this the dominant position forecast by the proponents of the service economy, the economy in which the process of producing services outweighs manufacturing production?

4 Where Does This Leave Us?

We can see the implications of the findings of the previous two sections by comparing the size of the U.K. service employment with its consumption of services – see Table 5.11. The proportion of service consumption to the total of final consumption is

TABLE 5.11 *Comparison of service consumption with service employment in the United Kingdom, 1954–74*

	1954	1961	1966	1971	1974
Service employment as percentage of total	34.5	38.7	41.3	45.3	48.1
Services as percentage of current expenditure	16.4	18.2	19.6	21.1	22.5
(Services as percentage of real consumption in 1954 terms)	(16.4)				(19.6)

considerably less than half of the proportion of service employees to total employment. Furthermore, when we separate education and medicine as categories of employment and consumption. (Table 5.12), we see that the remaining categories of service employment are even more disproportionate to the consumption of services than would appear from the previous table. The conclusion is inescapable: though the growth in demand for some

TABLE 5.12 *Comparison between medicine and education, and other service activities, 1954–74*

	1954	1961	1966	1971	1974
Employment in medicine and education	6.2	7.8	9.3	11.2	12.7
Expenditure on medicine and education	7.1	8.4	8.7	9.2	11.1
Employment in other service industries	28.3	30.9	32.0	34.1	35.4
Expenditure on other services	9.3	9.8	10.9	11.9	11.4

services may be sufficient to explain the growth of some individual categories of service employment, in general we must look elsewhere for such explanations. The relatively small total of service consumption, and the uncertainty and frequent reverses in the trends of individual service items, make growth in such consumption an unconvincing explanation for the steady and sizeable growth to be observed in employment in service occupations. Presumably, 35 per cent of the working population is not engaged in supplying 11 per cent of final consumption. So what are they doing?

We have three possible explanations which we shall examine in some detail in the following chapter, and which may each contain a germ of the truth. The first of these is really no more than a restatement of the phenomenon: when we examine the detailed pattern of growth within individual service occupational categories, we find that it consists predominantly of increased employment in occupations contributing to the final consumption of goods, rather than of services. We will see that, in 1974, nearly one-quarter of all service workers were concerned with selling or insuring goods. We will see that the fastest-growing professional group is engineers and other related technical workers, that there has been a continuous increase in the employment of service workers in manufacturing industry, and that there does seem to be some correlation between productivity and the level of service employment. We must be wary of attributing causes – in a complex system, all elements are linked, and the attempt to identify any subset of them as primary or driving forces must be fallacious; so the enrolment of educational and medical occupations among those groups instrumental to material production would probably force the argument past its natural limits. Nevertheless, within these limits it does constitute a consistent point of view: a significant proportion of the growth in service employment contributes directly to the efficiency of the production of goods, and is not directly concerned in the provision of services for final consumption.

This first really constitutes no more than a redefinition of the problem – it goes no way to telling us why service occupations should increase, other than the assertion of the contribution to productivity. The second explanation does go some way to supplying this lack; service occupations are asserted to be in some way better – more hygienic, less alienating, more stimulating – than others. This argument involves one of two alternative causal sequences. The simpler is that espoused by the majority of our improvement theorists (Bell, Dahrendorf, Schumacher): that as society moves from economic to sociological criteria in the design and development of economic institutions, so we will be able to 'improve' jobs, even at the cost of productivity, and this improvement will include the extension of service employment. This, of course, assumes that services are relatively unproductive of tangible goods, and hence – and quite contrary to the evidence – that they would not grow of their own accord within a capitalist economy; in fact, we find growth in service employment within the privately-owned sections of manufacturing industry as in public provision of social services. So we can only incline towards the second version of this explanation; that 'improved' jobs, including services, are necessary to attract and motivate the now 'affluent' workforce. With generally full employment levels, and generous unemployment payments, the increased cost of providing more satisfying jobs may be more than offset by reductions in losses accruing from absenteeism and job turnover, and from improved efficiency of job performance.

The third explanation is rather more cynical; instead of attributing real benefits to service employment, it asserts simply that autonomous institutional dynamics lead to the growth of service occupations – particularly administrative jobs – irrespective of their contribution to the output of the institution. This view stems ultimately from Weber's 'Iron Law of Bureaucracy'; Etzioni and Galbraith each have their own version of it, but perhaps the most succinct statement of it comes from the English historian and humorist, C. Northcote Parkinson:[1]

Work expands so as to fill the time available for its completion. . . . there need be little or no relationship between the work to be done and the size of the staff to which it may be assigned . . . 'an official wants to multiply subordinates, not rivals' . . . 'officials make work for each other'. (Parkinson, *Parkinson's Law*, pp. 11–12)

This vision of 'an economy based on reading each other's

minutes' is one shared by proponents and critics of the service society, and does again constitute a tenable, partial explanation of the phenomena we have under consideration.

We will be able to provide some evidence for each of these explanations – service occupations as instrumental in the production of goods, service occupations as inherently more satisfying jobs, and the service sector as the autonomously burgeoning bureaucracy empty of benefit to society – sufficient to suggest that each may contribute to the answer, and such that jointly, they amount to a much more satisfactory explanation of the growth of service occupations than Bell's suggestion of the growth of demand for the final consumption of services. But before we continue with the discussion of these explanations, we should pause to reassess the 'service economy' thesis in the light of the arguments and data presented in this chapter.

5 Goods or Services?

We have, in the previous two chapters, adduced two basic objections to the service economy thesis.

(1) It fails to make a clear distinction between the final consumption of 'services' and employment in 'service occupations' or 'service industries'. While the consumption of services requires service workers, the contrary is untrue – service workers do not necessarily produce services.

(2) It assumes that particular needs require services for their fulfilment; we have seen, on the contrary, a consistent pattern of replacement of services by goods.

The service economy thesis, reduced to essentials, runs thus: 'by extending Engel's Law we predict an increase in the consumption of services with increasing income, which must lead to an increase of service employment; we do indeed find evidence of such an increase in service employment, and hence we are moving towards the service economy'. At a purely formal level there is an error of logic, an invalidly reversed implication, that though services lead to service employment, service employment does not necessarily lead to services. This formal, potential error becomes a reality when we observe that with the exception of medicine and health, expenditure on services has actually fallen in the United Kingdom and other developed economies over the last twenty years. This must constitute a reasonably convincing rebuttal of the service economy thesis as an explanation of recent historical change.

However, Bell and other theorists are concerned with more than the historical explanation; their ultimate intentions are to make a forecast. Have we anything with which to replace this vision of the future of society dominated by the provision of services and amenities? We do have an alternative generalisation to propose. The first part of it has already been made explicit: service occupations – and here we are talking principally about managerial, technical and professional occupations – have increased in the past for a combination of reasons (their productivity, their inherent preferability as jobs, and the operation of 'Parkinson's Law'), and since these reasons continue to hold, we can only expect this growth to continue into the future. The second part concerns service consumption; in direct contradiction to Bell, we can identify a decreasing trend for the consumption of services.

The extension of Engel's Law to apply to services is mistaken, because, as we have shown, particular needs are not specific to either goods or services, and the manner of their provision may change over time. In order to make a generalisation about the future balance between goods and services, we need to identify some systematic attribute of the process by which newly emerging needs are answered by means of provision. The most obvious aspect of this process seems to point in the direction suggested by Bell; the more distant the needs are from the basic necessities, the more abstract and complicated they are likely to be, and the more difficult to mechanise, and hence the more likely to be provided for by services rather than by goods. Why, then, do we observe a move away from services?

The answer takes us back to the fundamental nature of services. Their essence is their personal nature – at the simplest a one-to-one relationship between servant and served – for Bell, services are 'a game between people', unmediated by 'things'. Now, in an economy with considerable disparities of income, we find two things: first, a disparity of needs, the rich having, at the margin, needs for complicated and abstract luxuries, the poor for basic necessities; second, the rich are able to buy the full-time services of the poor. In such a situation we would predict that the luxury needs of the rich would be met by services – that they would employ full-time servants to supply them. But as the members of a society become individually richer, and as incomes and wealth become more evenly distributed, two things will happen; first, fewer people will be willing to undertake menial tasks, to be literally at someone's 'beck and call'; second, marginal needs will become more similar and more people will be demanding these complicated and abstract luxuries. Though the cultural requirements of the readers of this chapter may approximate to those of an eighteenth-century Prince Esterhazy, they are more likely than he to possess a stereophonic record player, and less likely to employ Haydn and a full orchestra.

Now, some services, education, for example, or theatre, though still 'personal', are not 'one-to-one' but 'one-to-many'. The foregoing argument still applies insofar as rising real wage rates for service workers make their product more expensive, but its force as an argument is weakened because the cost of the service is shared. Here another tendency emerges, a growing demand for individuality and personal choice. Concert programmes and language lessons cannot be precisely adjusted to the needs and desires of every auditor, but teaching machines and gramophone record collections can do precisely that. So, taking this tendency to demand individual choice – 'the new liberty' as Dahrendorf puts it – together with the implications of increasing equality of income, we might predict a trend away from services, towards goods. Certainly, as we observed above, provision for newly emerging needs is difficult – but technology does advance, and one reasonably straightforward way of viewing the path of advancing technology is precisely the progressive mechanisation of activities which formerly required the intervention of human skills – the replacement of services by goods.

Let us consider finally Bell's most forthright prediction in the passage quoted at the beginning of the previous chapter, the future growth in the consumption of medical and educational facilities, which he considers the quintessential services. Considered as history, these are, as we have seen, the only services which have grown over the last two decades; can we, as Bell tells us, expect them to continue to grow? Now, certainly as we get richer, we are more concerned about our health and our education, but this is not the issue. Rather, we should be asking whether these newly dominant needs will be met by goods or by services. Of course, the provision for these complicated needs by goods is not yet possible, but at least in education it is not very far off. It would only take some relatively minor technological developments (cheaper video machines and image storage media) to convert the U.K. 'Open University' system into a complete university education which could be bought, once and for all, over the counter of some educational emporium. To take just one example, consider this statement from the Director of the National Extension College:

> The characteristics of an open-learning system are that the learning opportunity is available to any person, at any level, at any time, in any place, and in any subject . . . you should be able to do Chinese at three o'clock in the morning in a Welsh mountain village, or learn multiplication tables at 4 p.m. in central Birmingham . . . an open learning system must be built on materials – print, tape, kits – and the student must be able to control his use of them. The teacher of course is still there. He is needed to man the base where the resources are, to run classes for those who want them, to run tutorials, to mark correspondence assignments, to make up courses from material banks and to provide a diagnostic and advisory service. (Richard Freeman, in *The Listener*, 14 October 1976)

This, all things considered, is a much more likely picture of future 'lifelong, continuing education', than Bell's image of the ramifying university, the coming of the predominant don; an emphasis on educational 'material', with the teacher as a sort of maintenance engineer, a system achieving, not just high productivity from trained manpower, but also, however repugnant to the values of those in more traditional education, a high degree of flexibility to the needs of the user, catering, in fact, for Dahrendorf's new liberty.

Medicine is not so far advanced, but then, if there were no powerful lobbies interested in preventing it, over how distant a horizon would be the diagnostic and prescribing machine? Twenty years? . . . Fifty years? Whichever the answer, it will lie within the same distance forward into the future as we have considered back into the past in this and the previous chapter.

We cannot say for certain, as Bell asks us to, that the same social forces that produced the home washing machine and the home music machine, will not in the future produce the home hospital machine or the home university.

We have to say that, with increasing societal equality of incomes, and increasing desire for 'the new liberty' of choice, the expenditure on services as a proportion of income is likely to decrease, while that on goods increases, and since, for similar reasons, the price of services rises faster than that of goods, the real consumption of services will decline faster than the expenditure proportion. The data discussed in section 2 of this chapter shows precisely this pattern of change in the United Kingdom over the last twenty years.

As a prediction, however, this statement needs a caveat; we have not provided any evidence to suggest that this trend is inevitable, that there is no possible action that would steer us away from goods, and towards the service economy. Without wishing to get ahead of the argument, we can observe a number of reasons why we should want a service economy – it might bring lesser demand for irreplaceable resources, fairness to the worst-off members of the society, quality of life improvements – and hence, that we should want the state to manipulate the workings of the system to bring about such an economy. The conclusion to these chapters is devoted precisely to arguing that some such action may be desirable. Our present purpose is, however, simply to contend that the development of the service economy is not inevitable and independent of political decision, and therefore, that the capitalist ethic will not edge of its own accord into a 'communal' one, that on the present evidence, and in the absence of any contrary action, the future of our society lies not, as Bell suggests, in the provision of services and amenities, but rather, as now, in the provision and consumption of ever more goods. The changes we have been observing, from services to goods, or possibly from capital investment in manufacturing industry to capital investment in the home, may be best summarised not as the 'service economy', but as the 'self-service' economy.[2]

CHAPTER SIX

SERVICE EMPLOYMENT AND MATERIAL PRODUCTION

1 Productivity and the Tertiary Sector

In the previous two chapters we have identified both a trend towards service employment and a trend away from the final consumption of services. We have argued that there is in fact no contradiction here, only a confusion which arises from the use of the word 'service' in two different senses. One result of this confusion has been the view that since, to paraphrase Adam Smith, 'services . . . perish in the very instant of their performance', the contribution of service workers to economic welfare is necessarily inconsiderable; if Britain's problem is 'too few producers', then, according to this view, the continued growth of the service sector can only worsen our problem. The intention in this chapter is to show that this position is false.

The argument put forward here is simply that the growth of the service sector of employment, and of service occupations, is largely a manifestation of the process of the division of labour. The planning, forecasting, organisational functions are removed from the individual artisans and passed to other workers whose functions lie entirely within these areas, and who are not directly involved in the physical manipulation of materials; hence the growth of 'white collar' clerical, administrative, management occupations. The pattern of commerce becomes more geographically diffuse, the volume of international trade grows, the time span of the productive process from initial investment to final sales lengthens, so banking, insurance and other financial institutions account for a growing proportion of employment. The physical process of production becomes more technical, and so more dependent on those with technological expertise, and thus indirectly on the educational system which promotes this expertise. And, arguably, as part of this process, increasing alienation in the workforce brought about by the division of labour leads to a requirement for better welfare facilities, health care and education.

Adam Smith, in the passage quoted in Chapter 4, clearly identified merchants as integral parts of the system of material production; we are merely applying this principle . . . in concert with another drawn from the same source:

> . . . there are also some callings, which, though useful and even necessary in a state bring no advantage or pleasure to any individual, and the supreme power is obliged to . . . give them public encouragement in order to their subsistence . . . The persons employed in the finances, fleets and magistracy, are instances of this order of men. (Smith, *Wealth of Nations*, ch. 1, pp. 311–12)

The smooth functioning of the productive system requires, in addition to those who make an identifiable contribution to a particular productive process (whether direct or indirect), and who may be paid on that basis, others who make no such directly identifiable contribution, but who are nevertheless necessary for the progress of the economy – in modern terms, public administrators or teachers, clergymen or social workers. The weight of the argument in this chapter is, however, on the former of these categories, on those service workers who make an identifiable contribution to the manufacturing process.

2 Changes in Industrial Employment

In aggregate between 1961 and 1971 there was a small fall in total employment in manufacturing industry, amounting to 4 per cent of the 1961 G.B. workforce, and approximately 10 per cent of manufacturing employment – see Table 6.1. This aggregate fall in employment does not imply that all the individual industries have been declining; as we look through the list we see that food, coal products, chemicals, electrical engineering, paper-making and printing, metal manufacturing, and other manufacturing, have all increased their levels of employment, whereas the other ten categories have decreased employment. Primary employment has shown a considerable decline over the period – see Table 6.2. The total decrease here amounts to 2.5 per

TABLE 6.1   *Change in employment in manufacturing industry, 1961–71*

Industrial orders (1971 classification)	1971 as % of 1961 employment	% of G. B. workforce*	
		1961	1971
Food	105	3.1	3.2
Coal products	101	0.3	0.3
Chemicals	104	1.9	2.0
Metal manufacture	88	2.7	2.4
Mechanical engineering	100	4.9	4.8
Instrument engineering	101	0.6	0.6
Electrical engineering	111	3.3	3.6
Shipbuilding	76	1.0	0.8
Vehicles	94	3.7	3.4
Metal goods n.c.c.	112	2.3	2.5
Textiles	75	3.5	2.5
Leather and fur	87	0.3	0.2
Clothing and footwear	86	2.4	2.0
Bricks, etc.	95	1.4	1.3
Timber	99	1.3	1.3
Paper, printing, etc.	101	2.7	2.6
Other manufacturing	110	1.3	1.4
All manufacturing	95	36.8	34.9

*Working population excluding H. M. Forces throughout

TABLE 6.2   *Change in employment in primary industries, 1961–71*

	1971 as % of 1961 employment	% of G.B. workforce	
		1961	1971
Agriculture, forestry, fishing	74	3.7	2.7
Mining, quarrying	54	3.1	1.7
All primary	65	6.8	4.4

cent of the U.K. workforce, a larger proportional decline than that in all manufacturing industry over the decade, which constitutes a 35 per cent reduction on the 1961 employment level. We should bear in mind that this scale of decline need not bring any personal hardship. Ten years is, after all, one-fifth of a working life, so that in declining industries we would expect that more than 20 per cent of those in employment at the beginning of a decade would have left the working population altogether by the end of it. Adding voluntary changes in job during the working life to this, we can see how this decline in employment could be comfortably achieved through a process of natural wastage. So though there may be unfortunate local effects, this decline in employment – which has been accompanied both in mining and in agriculture by increasingly intensive use of capital – has not necessarily been the occasion of widespread individual suffering.

In the intermediate category, employment has remained largely constant – see Table 6.3. The main change here is in transport and communications. The apparent 7 per cent fall hides a 50 per cent decline in employment on the railways, which is largely counterbalanced by increases in employment in road haulage and telecommunications.

TABLE 6.3   *Change in employment in intermediate industry, 1961–71*

	1971 as % of 1961 employment	% of G. B. workforce	
		1961	1971
Construction	104	7.0	7.2
Utilities	96	1.6	1.6
Transport and communications	93	7.3	6.7
All intermediate	98	15.9	15.4

This leaves us with an approximate overall decline of 5 per cent in employment in primary, secondary and intermediate employment, and a 5 per cent increase in the 'unproductive' tertiary sector. (These percentages are only approximate because of the number of unallocated categories in the census returns – 0.3 per cent in 1961, and 0.7 per cent of the working population in 1971.) Table 6.4 shows that all the service industry categories, except distribution, have grown over the period. The fastest growth is seen in banking and finance, which have increased their employment by more than half, whereas miscellaneous services, which, following Bell we might have expected to have grown, have stayed almost constant in absolute size and fallen as a proportion of the U.K. workforce. As we saw in the previous chapter, U.K. household consumption of the product of this

TABLE 6.4   *Change in employment in tertiary industry, 1961–71*

	1971 as % of 1961 employment	% of G.B. workforce	
		1961	1971
Distribution	95	13.9	12.9
Financial	166	2.5	4.1
Professional and scientific	137	9.2	12.4
Miscellaneous services	97	9.9	9.6
Public administration	146	4.9	6.3
All tertiary	114	40.4	45.8

industry has fallen, and employment in it would presumably have fallen further were it not for the growth in tourism over the period.

But the important thing to notice about this group of five industries is that though none of them directly produces material goods, a sizeable proportion of their employment is closely connected with the process of production in its slightly wider sense. The distribution industry, for instance, does not itself make any material object, and yet is an integral part of the process of making things. If products cannot be sold, then they will not be produced, and as we have seen, Adam Smith insists that 'merchants' are to be considered equally as productive as 'artisans'. Similarly, the major part of finance and insurance is taken up with facilitating the production or purchase of goods. Among those employed in the professional and scientific sector, though a majority are educational, medical or social workers, still a minority – engineers and technologists, members of the liberal professions such as lawyers, accountants and architects – are really involved in the provision of material goods rather than immaterial services – see Table 6.5. Public administration is rather difficult to classify in this manner. Certainly, many Government departments – for example, the Department of Industry – would be concerned to see their role as that of fostering material productivity, whereas others – the Department of the Environment, or the Department of Health and Social Security – are certainly more concerned with the provision of services rather than goods. But other Ministries are more difficult to place, and in any case, even the apparently clear attributions will

TABLE 6.5 *Professional and scientific services – goods-related?*

	1961	1971		1961	1971
Educational services	3.8	5.9	Service-related	7.5	10.4
Medical and dental	3.4	4.2			
Religious organisations	0.3	0.3			
Accountancy	0.4	0.4	Goods-related	1.7	2.0
Legal services	0.4	0.5			
Research and scientific	0.9	1.1			

blur on closer investigation; so, for the purposes of the following calculation, we shall hold public administration separate from the first four categories.

On the basis of these attributions, we can calculate the proportion of tertiary industrial employment which is more closely related to goods than to services[1] – see Table 6.6. Taking all distribution and financial workers together with liberal professionals and technical workers as being essentially goods-related, we find that these categories take up around half of the employment in tertiary industries. The proportion has fallen a little over the period, but employment in this category has grown absolutely, and the size of the growth trend is somewhat disguised by the contraction in employment in distribution. This is in itself a microcosm of the society-wide goods-in-place-of-services substitution which is our central theme, replacing the labour intensive corner shop with the capital intensive, machine-dependent supermarket or hypermarket. Furthermore, if we attribute equal parts of the employment in Public Administration to the two categories, we can estimate the proportions for

TABLE 6.6 *Tertiary industry–goods or services?*

	1961		1971	
Goods-related: distribution, financial, part of professional and scientific	18.1		19.0	
Plus half of public administration		20.5		22.2
Service-related: miscellaneous services, part of professional and scientific	17.4		20.0	
Plus half of public administration		19.8		23.2
		40.3		45.4

the whole of tertiary industry. We find that this still leaves little short of a majority of tertiary industry employees in goods-related employment. So, in 1971, though nearly a half of the working population was employed in the tertiary sector, less than a quarter of it – 23.1 per cent – was involved in providing for the final consumption of services.

1971 is the latest date for which we have the reliable Population Census estimates. We can get a less reliable glimpse into subsequent changes from the Census of Occupation – see Table 6.7. The largest part of the growth in service-related tertiary employment is in education and medicine, a trend which we do not anticipate will continue, particularly given permanent cuts in the level of teacher-training. Nevertheless, we appear on the threshold of Daniel Bell's post-industrial transition: 'the first and simplest definition of a post-industrial society is that the

TABLE 6.7   *Employment in the United Kingdom: goods and services, 1971 and 1975*

	1971		1975	
Primary, secondary, intermediate		54.7		49.3
Tertiary: goods-related	21.8		22.7	
service-related	23.4		28.0	
		45.3		50.7
		100.0		100.0

majority of the labour force is no longer engaged in agriculture or manufacturing, but in services'.[2] But, we argue in this chapter, this says nothing about a 'service economy' – hardly more than a quarter are involved in service-providing industry, and by the arguments in the previous chapter, we would expect this proportion to decrease in the future.

3   Occupations – Goods- or Services-Related?

So far we have only been talking about employment classified by industry, which does not give us all the necessary information. The industrial classification gives a guide as to the main activity of the employing firm, rather than the occupation of the employee. In this section, we will undertake a similar exercise to the previous investigation of the proportion of the tertiary sector actually engaged in the production of services, but in this case on rather more informative data that tells us what jobs people actually do. We shall start by considering the relationship between the occupational and industrial employment distributions, classified for the moment according to the conventional sectors. A very powerful tool for this purpose is provided by the cross-tabulations in the 1961 and 1971 Census, of industrial employment against occupation. It tells us, for each category of final output, how many of which categories of jobs went into its production. We can start by considering a very highly summarised version of the 1971 tables – see Table 6.8.[3]

Two particularly interesting observations emerge from these tables. The first is that a very small proportion of the working population actually have 'shopfloor' jobs in manufacturing industry. We see that only 18.6 per cent of the workforce, a bare majority of manufacturing workers, are employed in manufacturing processes in manufacturing industry. In order to estimate the numbers directly concerned in the direct manipulation of material, to revert to the definition of 'goods-producing' occupations used in the previous chapter, we should perhaps add the unskilled labourers in manufacturing industry included in the 'intermediate' occupational category (approximately 2.3 per cent of the workforce); this gives us a total of approximately 21 per cent of the working population directly involved in the production of goods. The second observation is the very large proportion of working population (37.9 per cent) in tertiary occupations in the tertiary industrial sector. If we look at the sixteen industrial/occupational categories in the above tables, we find that the two largest categories are 'secondary industry/ secondary occupation' and 'tertiary industry/tertiary occupation' which together account for more than 56 per cent of the workforce, and we see that the service component of this group is more than twice as large as the manufacturing one. To take an alternative indicator, the sum of all workers in either (or both) tertiary industries and tertiary occupations, is 59.5 per cent, whereas the proportion in secondary industries or occupations is 41.1 per cent. Whichever the indicator, the service worker is clearly more typical of the U.K. average than is the manufacturing worker.

Table 6.9 shows the equivalent figures for 1961. The clearest

TABLE 6.8 *Distributions of occupations across industry, 1971*

Industrial sector	Occupational sector				
	Primary Agriculture, fishing, mining	*Secondary* Skilled and semi-skilled, manufacturing	*Intermediate* Construction, transport, etc., unskilled labour	*Tertiary* Administrative, technical, clerical, etc.	*Total* in industrial sector
As percentage of total workforce					
Primary Mining, farming	3.5	0.3	0.3	0.35	4.4
Secondary Manufacturing	0.5	18.6	6.2	10.0	34.9
Intermediate Transport, utilities, construction	0.3	3.4	8.1	3.8	15.4
Tertiary Administrative, finance, technical	0.5	2.9	3.8	37.9	45.3
As percentage of workforce in each sector					
Primary	78.4	7.0	6.5	7.9	
Secondary	0.1	53.3	17.8	28.6	
Intermediate	0.2	22.1	52.6	24.8	
Tertiary	1.2	6.4	8.4	83.7	

TABLE 6.9 *Distribution of occupations across industries, 1961*

| | Occupations | | | | | | | | |
| | as % of workforce | | | | | as % of sector | | | |
Industries	Prim.	Sec.	Interm.	Tert.	Total	Prim.	Sec.	Interm.	Tert.
Primary	5.7	0.4	0.4	0.4	6.9	82.9	5.2	5.8	5.5
Secondary	0.1	20.1	6.8	9.2	36.6	0.1	54.9	18.5	25.1
Intermediate	0.3	3.3	9.3	3.2	15.9	0.2	20.6	58.3	19.8
Tertiary	0.5	3.1	4.0	32.6	40.6	1.4	7.6	9.9	80.3

trend to be observed over the decade is the increase of tertiary jobs in secondary, intermediate, and tertiary industry. The fastest growth is in intermediate industry, where the tertiary occupational employment has risen by 5 per cent (from 19.8 per cent to 24.8 per cent) of all employment. The increase of tertiary occupations from 25.1 per cent to 28.6 per cent of manufacturing employment is slightly larger than the rise in occupational employment in tertiary industry, even though in absolute terms around three-quarters of those in service occupations are employed in tertiary industry. But, as we noted in the previous section, much of tertiary industry is goods- rather than services-related; we must again try to separate this portion out from the total.

We can start by considering the tertiary occupational classification in 1961 and 1971 in relation to the other sectors. Looking at occupations (Table 6.10), we see that we had already crossed the 50 per cent tertiary transition by 1971. But, as we can see from

TABLE 6.10 *Occupations in the United Kingdom, 1961 and 1971*

		1961	1971	$\frac{1971}{1961}$
All primary, intermediate, secondary		53.5	47.4	0.89
Tertiary	Clerical	13.3	14.9	1.12
	Sales	9.8	9.3	0.95
	Services	10.5	12.2	1.16
	Administration	2.8	3.9	1.39
	Professional and technical	8.9	11.5	1.29
All tertiary		45.3	51.8	1.14

the occupational/industrial cross-tabulation (Table 6.11), a large proportion of many in the tertiary occupational classification are, in fact, employed either in manufacturing industry, or in goods-related industry (distribution, banking, insurance and finance).

TABLE 6.11   *Tertiary occupations and their employment, 1961–71*

		1961	1971	1971 ÷ 1961
Clerical	Manufacturing	6.0	6.0	1.00
	Goods-related	3.4	4.2	1.24
	Services-related	3.9	4.7	1.20
Sales	Manufacturing	0.9	0.9	1.00
	Goods-related	8.4	7.9	0.99
	Services-related	0.5	0.5	1.00
Services	Manufacturing	1.4	2.1	1.50
	Goods-related	0.5	0.8	1.40
	Services-related	8.7	10.1	1.16
Administration	Manufacturing	1.9	2.5	1.32
	Goods-related	0.3	0.6	2.00
	Services-related	0.6	0.8	1.33
Professional and technical	Manufacturing	2.5	3.2	1.28
	Goods-related	0.5	0.5	1.00
	Services-related	6.0	7.8	1.30

When we add together each of the three employment categories across the five occupational classifications, we find that manufacturing together with goods-related occupations constitute the clear majority (Table 6.12). Only 46 per cent of those in tertiary occupations are engaged in the provision of

TABLE 6.12   *Industrial employment of tertiary sectoral occupations, 1961–71*

		1961	1971	1971 ÷ 1961
	Manufacturing	11.5	13.9	1.18
	Goods-related	14.2	14.0	0.99
All tertiary				
	Manufacturing and goods	25.7	27.9	1.13
	Service-related	19.7	23.9	1.21

services. Using the original sectoral classification, we saw that in the 1971 occupational/industrial cross-tabulation, 37.9 per cent of the working population fell into the tertiary industrial/tertiary occupational cell. We can now see that more than one-third of those (14 per cent of the working population) are engaged in goods-related activities, leaving only 23.9 per cent of the working population engaged in the provision of services.

However, even this is an over-estimate, since a proportion of the professional and technical occupations, while not directly employed by manufacturing or manufacturing-related industries, still contribute to material productivity. To complete this analysis we will look in a little more detail at the professional occupations. To start with, we can select a number of individual professional and technical occupations (Table 6.13). We have

TABLE 6.13 *Examples of growth in selected professional and technical occupations, 1961–71 (growth shown in thousands)*

	1961	1971	1971 / 1961
Technical and related (n.c.c.)	76	196	2.55
Mechanical engineers	48	98	2.02
University teachers	14	27	1.91
Social workers	41	68	1.66
Clergy	61	41	0.67

taken here the fastest-growing four occupations, and the fastest-declining of the occupations. We see that the two fastest-growing groups, technical and related workers (this must be mostly computer programmers who do not have a separate classification) and mechanical engineers, both goods-related occupations, are largely concerned in some phase of the process of production. The next fastest-growing group is that of university teachers, certainly service workers, but not very large numbers in absolute terms, and, sadly, not increasing in number at this rate in the 1970s. Next come social workers, who are in absolute terms rather a large group and certainly still growing . . . but, if we look at the fastest-declining group, the clergymen, we find that the absolute fall is of roughly the same order of magnitude as the rise of social workers, and to the extent that their duties, or at least the temporal aspect of them, are similar, the aggregate increase in the two occupations is only very small.

This, of course, is very much selected evidence. To get a more general picture we can consider the entire technical and professional occupational order, allocated into seven sub-categories as shown in Table 6.14. Here we see that by far the

TABLE 6.14 *Growth in all professional and technical occupational groups, 1961–71, shown as percentage of the working population*

	1961	1971	1971 / 1961
Medical workers	2.04	2.51	1.23
Teachers	2.21	2.90	1.31
Engineers, etc.	1.13	1.67	1.48
Artists, etc.	0.43	0.52	1.21
Liberal professions	1.36	1.59	1.17
Technical auxiliaries	1.20	1.18	0.98
Other technical	0.51	1.12	2.12
All professional and technical	8.89	11.49	1.29

fastest-growing group is again that which contains computer programmers and other technical personnel. The next fastest-growing group is engineers, whose numbers have increased by almost one-half over the decade. The rate of growth in teachers' numbers is only slightly faster than the average for technical and professional occupations, and all the other obviously service-related occupations are increasing at slower than the average rate. The technical auxiliary category, which apparently runs counter to the trends we are trying to exhibit, is in fact subject to depletion because of technical and social innovation. This category includes draughtsmen and laboratory assistants, many of whose more repetitive and less-skilled activities have been replaced by computers, computer-driven plotting mach-ines, and other automatic machinery. From this breakdown we can divide the order into its goods-related and service-related components – see Table 6.15.

Thus, even without the arbitrary division of liberal pro-fessions, we can see that the goods-related proportion of pro-fessional occupations has increased over the period, that in 1971 about 42 per cent of those falling into this order were goods-

TABLE 6.15   *Professional occupations in goods and services, 1961–71*

	1961	1971	1971/1961
Goods-related: engineers, technical, etc.	2.85	3.98	1.40
Plus half of liberal professions	3.53	4.77	1.35
Service-related: medical, teachers, artists	4.68	5.93	1.27
Plus half of liberal professions	5.36	6.72	1.25
	8.89	11.49	1.29

related, and that the rate of growth in goods-related professional occupations is considerably faster than that of service-related. So, going back to our table examining the employment of workers in tertiary occupations, we have to amend the estimate of service-related professional and technical occupations to take account of the various engineers, technologists, and other professionals who are self-employed, and thus appear in a service industry, but who nevertheless contribute directly to material production. This category is therefore reduced by 1.1 per cent to 6.7 per cent of the working population which in turn reduces the total of all tertiary occupations in service-related industry to 22.8 per cent, which compares quite closely to the estimate we derived from the industrial data, and is also very close to the estimate in the previous chapter of the proportion of national expenditure on services.

4   Too Few Producers?

Considerable attention has recently been devoted to the growth of the service sector in the U.K. economy as a result of a book by Robert Bacon and Walter Eltis, *Britain's Economic Problem: Too Few Producers*.[4] They discuss three different explanations for Britain's current problem; the first of these, and possibly for that reason the most frequently quoted of them, is what they consider to be the disproportionate rise in the provision of services:

Virtually all modern economies gradually shift workers out of industry and into services as industrial efficiency rises, and aspirations grow for better education and welfare services, as well as for the many services provided in the private sector. They do not, however, have (as Britain has) 34 per cent shifts in just thirteen years, and cannot without great strain. (Bacon and Eltis, *Britain's Economic Problem*, p. 12, parenthesis added)

They argue that the alleged strain of expansion of services is at least a contributing factor to the present British malaise. There are, however, a number of problems with their argument.

First, there is an element of exaggeration, statistically valid, but nevertheless misleading to the unwary, in their presentation. Consider, for example, the histogram (Figure 6.1) taken from

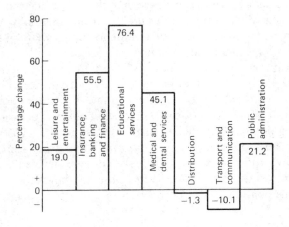

FIGURE 6.1   *Percentage change in service sector employment by category in the United Kingdom, 1961–74*

their book, which is intended to demonstrate the disproportionate size of growth of tertiary industry. The categories used here are sometimes Industrial Orders – that is, standard groupings of industries, such that distribution, for instance, constitutes the order containing 'wholesale distribution', 'retail distribution', 'dealing in coal, etc.' and 'dealing in other materials' – whereas educational services, and medical and dental services are simply industries within the order 'professional services'. If we do permit ourselves to pick and choose among categories in this way, and look only at growth rates, then we could just as well confound Bacon and Eltis by turning to the occupational statistics and pointing out that 'technical and related professions' and 'mechanical engineers' are growing in number, respectively, five and three times as fast as teachers (see Table 6.14). Of course, this is a statistic of limited usefulness, given that there are, in absolute terms, many more teachers than mechanical engineers and members of technical professions. If we want to discuss the structure of industry, we have to look both at rates of change and at absolute size of employment in the various categories – see Figure 6.2. The horizontal scale gives the relative employment

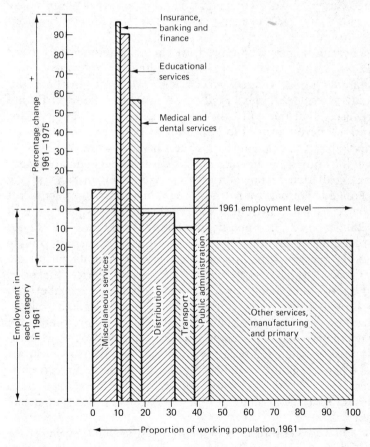

FIGURE 6.2   *Increase in service categories, shown in proportion to total employment, 1961–75*

proportions in 1961, the vertical scale indicates rates of growth, and the shaded areas give relative employment proportions in 1975. We see that rates of growth vary more or less inversely with the initial size of the categories. We see, in addition, that the largest tertiary category, distribution, is falling; that the fastest growing category, which is also the smallest absolutely, is the most closely associated with the manufacturing sector; that education, the next fastest, is likely, following the arguments in the previous chapter, to level off and then fall in the near future, and medicine certainly not to rise as fast as hitherto. Public administration does indeed have a fast rate of increase, but its absolute size is not all that large. The significance of the growth of tertiary industry is considerable, but should not be over-estimated.

Bearing Figure 6.2 in mind, we might reconsider Bacon and Eltis' statistic of a 34 per cent shift in employment from manufacturing industry to services: what exactly does this statistic refer to? The casual reader might be forgiven for not realising that the shift is in fact the 'percentage change in the ratio of non-industrial to industrial employment between 1961 and 1974'.[5] 34 per cent sounds like a big change; we could easily get the impression that one-third of the working population have changed from manufacturing to services – but in fact the real change is not nearly that large. The first thing to remember is that a 34 per cent shift is merely the sum of two 17 per cent changes going in opposite directions. In Figure 6.2 we see something approximating to Bacon and Eltis' 34 per cent shift in the 17 per cent reduction in 'other services, manufacturing and primary', which goes to increase the various service categories: the actual movement of jobs amounts only to 17 per cent of 1961 manufacturing employment, about one-and-a-half million people. And one-and-a-half million is hardly more than 6 per cent of the working population. So the 34 per cent shift – which is, it must be stressed, a perfectly valid statistic – refers to a transfer of 6 per cent of the total jobs from the manufacturing sector into services. This 6 per cent still represents a sizeable change, but a less-dramatic sounding one than the Bacon and Eltis 34 per cent shift.

The second problem with their analysis is that they ignore the possibility that service workers may have a direct impact on material productivity. In this chapter we have seen that roughly half of all tertiary employment is, in fact, much more closely bound up with the production of goods than with the provision of services for final consumption. We saw that around 23 per cent of all jobs in 1975 were in service industries, but in service industries supplying manufacturing industry rather than the final consumer. Manufacturing industry needs professional services, banking, insurance, distribution. These tertiary industrial groups are certainly involved in the productive process – but are they *themselves* productive, as claimed at the beginning of this chapter? There is no way of answering this question directly, but we may get a clue by considering the relationship between manufacturing productivity and service employment within manufacturing industry – see Figure 6.3. There does seem to be a positive connection: the more service occupations employed in the industry, the more productive it is. And large deviations from

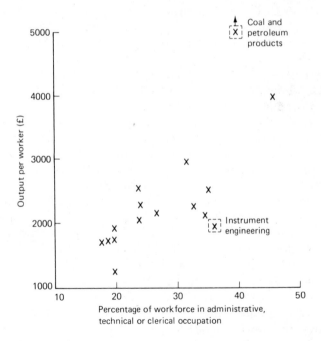

FIGURE 6.3 *Relationship between tertiary employment in manufacturing industries and output per head in the United Kingdom, 1970 (for the sixteen orders of manufacturing industry)*

the trend are easily explained by the nature of the individual
industries; petrol refining, for example, is a very advanced
continuous-process industry requiring very small input of labour,
whereas the highly technical nature of instrument engineering
leads to an unusual concentration of white collar workers. Of
course, we cannot specify the causal process involved here, but
we can certainly speculate that it indicates the productivity of
white-collar workers.

This is by no means a clinching argument, but the impact of
the service sector on material productivity is not something that
can be ignored, though Bacon and Eltis seem set against
recognising it even as a possibility. As an example of this,

> . . . many are prepared to believe that there is great wastage of
> resources in the public sector . . . In 1965–73, the adminis-
> trative staff in the National Health Service increased by 51 per
> cent while the number of beds occupied daily fell from 451,000
> to 400,000. There was one administrator or clerk to every 9.5
> beds in 1965 and one to every 5.6 occupied beds in 1973.
> (Bacon and Eltis, *Britain's Economic Problem*, pp. 84–5)

They are clearly recalling Parkinson's celebrated analysis of
growth in the Admiralty staff correlated with the decline in the
size of the Fleet. Yet only a moment's thought will reveal the
emptiness of the implied criticism. Is it, after all, necessarily a bad
sign that the number of occupied beds has been reduced? Could it
not be that as a matter of medical policy the average length of
stay of patients in hospitals is being curtailed? Might not then the
higher level of non-medical staff in the hospitals reflect the additional administrative burden imposed by this higher through-
put? In a rather similar way the possibility that such service
industries as banking, insurance, and distributive trades contribute to material productivity should at least be considered; Bacon
and Eltis do not take this possibility into account.

It should be added that in the longer term, other service sectors
may contribute to material production. This applies particularly
to education; manufacturing industry (as we shall see in the next
chapter) requires an increasingly skilled workforce, and with the
current rate of technical change, traditional methods of 'on-the-
job' training become increasingly inappropriate. We could spend

longer considering examples, but the general thrust of this second sort of objection to Bacon and Eltis' argument must by now be clear: they pay insufficient attention to the possibility that efficiency in manufacturing industry depends on employment in service industries.

The third class of objection is simply that the Bacon and Eltis approach does not sufficiently value the opportunity for employment in the service sector. Quite apart from the value of the services they provide, the tertiary sector provides jobs. In the next chapter we shall consider the likely reduction in demand for labour in manufacturing industry as a result of automation; the service sector, being relatively labour-intensive, may have provided a useful source of jobs, simply to keep people occupied. Bacon and Eltis would presumably object to this on the grounds that encouraging growth in the service sector damages the economy by attracting resources away from physical production. However, the available evidence seems to suggest that growth of output in the service sector does not inhibit manufacturing growth – see Figure 6.4. Far from being faced with a choice between growth in services and manufacturing, it appears that those countries with the fastest growth in services also have the

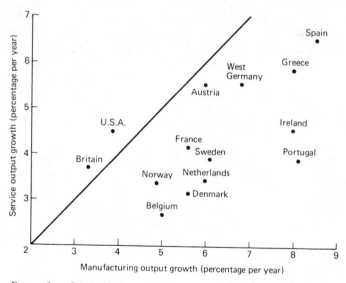

FIGURE 6.4 *Relationship between service and manufacturing output growth, 1953–67*

fastest rate of growth in manufacturing. Indeed, on this evidence it might be a rational strategy to encourage service employment to compensate for losses of manufacturing jobs due to technical advance and capital substitution.

The growth of the service sector is not the only thread to Bacon and Eltis' argument; they also talk of the problems caused by the increased production of non-marketable or non-tradable goods. They may be on firmer ground in suggesting these latter issues as causes of the United Kingdom's present problems, but certainly their proposal of the service sector as the scapegoat is unconvincing. They overstate the extent of its growth; they ignore the contribution it might make to material production; they assume against the evidence that it competes with manufacturing industry for scarce resources, whereas it may simply provide a useful source of employment for labour made redundant by increasingly efficient material production.

The main drift of this chapter is that it is impossible to view any industrial or occupational group as unproductive – even Adam Smith's bugbear, the clergyman, must be ceded some role in the chain of production. This raises a fundamental problem with the traditional 'sectoral' accounts of the economy; the type of accounting relationships described by input-output tables, for example, are extremely misleading as indicators of the actual functioning of the economic system. Reforming these systems of account is no part of our purpose here, however, so on the basis of the discussion in this chapter, we must limit ourselves to two observations. (1) Tertiary sector industrial and occupational groups are often integral parts of the system of material production, so that such descriptions as 'tertiary', 'service' and 'white-collar' may be confusing in discussions of the short-term behaviour of the system of material production; we need to develop more specific terms which relate more closely to the significance of particular employment groups to production. (2) The longer the time period we consider, the more employment groups must be brought into our conceptualisation of the productive system; for adequate prescription we will need to develop new models of economic structure, based on causal relationships between economic groups and institutions, rather than a simple and inevitably misleading monetary accounting of flows of goods and services.

To return to our central concern, we have shown that, in spite of the fact that about half of the working population is in tertiary occupations, less than quarter of it is actually engaged in the provision of services. We saw in the previous chapter that consumption of services by the population is not increasing in the way suggested by the service economy thesis; we have shown here that a considerable part of the growth in service employment, which the service economy's proponents explain as being the result of the transition from the final consumption of goods to that of services, is, on the contrary, to be explained as the result of the extension of the system of production of material goods.

CHAPTER SEVEN

WHAT HAPPENS TO JOBS?

1 Progress and the Degradation of Jobs

The next stage of the argument is the question of the nature of jobs in the changing economy. Does organisational and technical development mean that they are necessarily degraded over time? There are three alternative positions.

The first is an essentially optimistic position, one which extends right across the political spectrum. Consider a Marxist writer:

> . . . the whole nature of work itself would have changed. By the end of this century, we should be in the era of the fully automatic factory . . . there would be nothing left of mere manual labour or unskilled work or repetitive work. Every one of us would be doing a job that allowed him to use to the full all the skills of hand and brain with which he is endowed . . . the level of consumption of material commodities would be several times what it is today. A very much reduced labour force would be producing these commodities, largely in automatic factories. And they would be working a six- or a ten-hour week, at skilled and creative jobs. There would on the other hand be far larger numbers of scientists . . . probably the greatest increase of all would be in the numbers of people engaged in the teaching profession at all levels. (S. Lilley, *Automation and Social Progress*, p. 215)[1]

This is, of course, the prospect held out for a socialist Britain; but an only slightly less rosy, if more individualistically bracing image is projected by conservative writers. Consider, for example, another view from the 1950s:

> Industrial workers must realise that for them automation will bring not only a higher standard of living, more wages, more leisure and less fatiguing and health-destroying working-conditions, but also greatly improved opportunities for up-

grading. The best way to make them realise this is through a really impressive expansion of opportunities for technical education. This is essential to meet the increased need of engineers of various kinds and of highly skilled workers capable of operating automatic equipment. But it is an equally important consideration that such a development would multiply the opportunities of members of the working classes for bettering themselves over and above the general improvement expected of automation. (P. Einzig, *The Economic Consequences of Automation*, p. 213)[2]

The social processes envisaged by these two writers are, of course, quite different; but they have in common the prediction that within their chosen social system, automation will necessarily lead, through its own internal logic, to an improvement in the quality of life in general, and of working life in particular.

The second and third views are based precisely on the assumption that there are no such automatic secular tendencies for the protection of the quality of working life. The second is the pessimistic converse of the first, that under given social systems, the effect of technical progress is inevitably the degradation of jobs. This view is most widely encountered as a Marxist critique of capitalist economies, and we shall be drawing on one such source, Henry Braverman's *Monopoly Capital and the Labour Process*,[3] later in this chapter; but equally, such charges might be levelled at particular socialist countries, as in Huxley's paraphrase of Lenin's 'electricity plus socialism equals communism' as 'electricity plus heavy industry . . . equals misery, totalitarianism and war'. The defining characteristic of this position is the assumption that technologies in given social or political circumstances are inevitably malign in their effects. The third view, that of the liberal humanists whose 'improvement' theories are the basis of our investigation, is a modification of the second; technological change in its social context is seen as potentially malign, but avoidably so. Dahrendorf calls for 'technology assessment', Schumacher for the humanisation of job scale and content. The emphasis is on technical change as neither benign nor malign, but rather as a process in need of direction, not to be left to develop through its own logic in the marketplace, or in response to the demands of the planning system, but to be positively controlled in order to improve the quality of working life.

In this chapter, we shall consider these three views through theory and empirical evidence, with the intention of establishing whether the improvement of the stock of jobs – or, to be more precise, maintaining full employment whilst improving job satisfaction – in the United Kingdom may be safely left to the operation of the economic system, whether it requires a fundamental change in the system of ownership of capital as Braverman argues, or whether some meliorating extra-economic intervention in the structuring of jobs without such fundamental changes, following the liberal humanists, would achieve this aim.

2   Job Degradation and the Division of Labour

The division of labour is a powerful image for the process of change in the organisation of industry. The separation of the component tasks of a manufacturing process gives, as Adam Smith tells us, the following advantages:

> First, the improvement of the dexterity of the workman necessarily increases the quantity of work he can perform; and the division of labour, by reducing every man's business to some one simple operation, and by making this operation the sole employment of his life, necessarily increases very much the dexterity of the workman. . . . Secondly, the advantage which is gained by saving the time commonly lost in passing from one sort of work to another, is much greater than we should at first view be apt to imagine. . . . Thirdly, and lastly, everybody must be sensible how much labour is facilitated and abridged by the application of proper machinery . . . the invention of all those machines by which labour is so much facilitated and abridged, seems to have been originally owing to the division of labour. (Smith, *The Wealth of Nations*, pp. 11–13)

From these three categories, we conventionally derive the following conclusion: over time, employment of a highly skilled minority in vital technical and administrative occupations develops alongside a majority in increasingly structured, repetitive, boring and finally alienating tasks.

Charles Babbage[4] added a fourth advantage to the classical catalogue:

> ... the master manufacturer, by dividing the work to be executed into different processes, each requiring different degrees of skill or force, can purchase exactly that precise quantity of both which is necessary for each process; whereas, if the whole work were executed by one workman, that person must possess sufficient skill to perform the most difficult, and sufficient strength to execute the most laborious, of the operations into which the art is divided. (Babbage, *On the Economy of Machinery etc.*, pp. 175–6)

To illustrate this category of advantage, Babbage follows a distinguished precedent; he discusses a pin factory, examining the levels of skill and strength required in each of the component processes in the manufacture. He demonstrates that quite independent of the *technical* advantages, the wages for a workforce of a given size without division of labour would be three and one-quarter times as large as that with the application of the principle. This fourth category of advantage is not, however, as powerful as it might seem at first sight; the particular subdivided trades acquire their associated wage rates as a result of the divided manufacturing process; the wages of the highest paid trades in the pin factory ('tinning' at 6s per day, and 'pointing' at 5s 3d) do not necessarily represent the wages of the independent pin-maker, since those trades may themselves have been called into existence by the manufacturing process itself; but nevertheless, Babbage's addition to the theory has recently received some attention as the basis for pessimistic forecasts of the future employment patterns. The pessimistic conclusion does indeed emerge even more starkly from Babbage's addition than from Adam Smith's original argument; following Babbage, it pays industrialists to divide labour because, even independent of any technical advantages in the efficiency of labour, it has the effect of reducing the wage bill.

We can put the pessimistic conclusion more precisely, and into modern terms. We expect, given the advantages stemming from the division of labour, that the number of highly skilled technical, professional, and administrative workers, will grow, and grow at a rate rather slower than the rate of reduction in numbers of skilled manual workers. For each technical, professional or managerial worker gained, we would expect to lose more than one skilled manual worker and gain 'semi-skilled' or 'unskilled' workers accordingly. As Braverman puts it:

> The most common mode of cheapening labour power is exemplified by the Babbage principle: . . . Each step of the labour process is divorced, so far as possible, from special knowledge and training and reduced to simple labour. Meanwhile the relatively few persons for whom special knowledge and training are reserved are freed so far as possible from the obligations of simple labour. . . . This might be called the general law of the capitalist division of labour. (Braverman, *Labour and Monopoly Capital*, p. 82)

If we were to draw a graph with the percentage of the workforce in professional, managerial and technical occupations on the y-axis and percentage in skilled manual jobs on the x-axis, we should expect that for any society following the principle of division of labour a plot of the points it occupies over time would have a slope of between zero and -1 – see Figure 7.1. We do in fact have data to investigate this, from a special survey carried out by the National Insurance authorities between 1964 and 1968. Clerical workers are unfortunately classified together with professional, technical and managerial workers, but since we have independent evidence that employment of clerical workers in manufacturing industry has not risen at all since 1961 this does not affect our argument.[5] If we look first at proportions employed in factories of different sizes at one point in time, shown in Figure 7.2, we see that the slope of the line connecting the smallest to the largest is indeed less than -1. At any point in time, the larger the establishment, the more the logic of division of labour appears to be worked through and the proportion of technical, managerial and professional workers rises with size of firm but slower than the rate of fall of skilled manual workers.

But do we see a similar pattern when we look at change over time (Figure 7.3)? The actual pattern of change over this period is

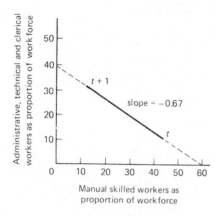

Our expectation is that, between time t and time $t + 1$, the decrease in the proportion of manual skilled workers should be larger than the increase in professional employees—that is, that the line connecting t and $t + 1$ should have a slope between 0 and −1

FIGURE 7.1 *The degradation of jobs – a graphical presentation*

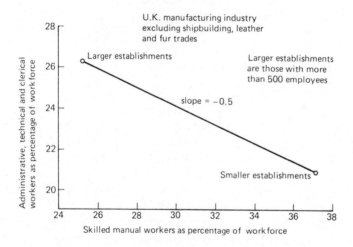

FIGURE 7.2 *Skilled manual and managerial employment in 1964*

therefore contrary to Braverman's prediction. We see that the cross-time slopes are considerably greater than − 1, which means that the total of managerial, technical and professional workers plus skilled manual workers is rising as a proportion of the workforce, and that the proportion of semi-skilled and unskilled workers is falling. And again, if we look at the absolute numbers

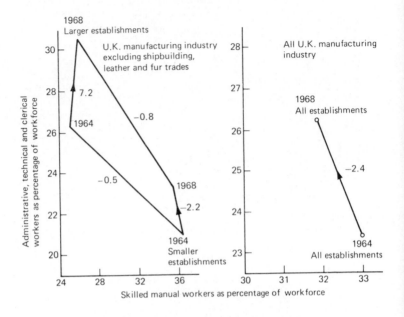

FIGURE 7.3   *Change in skilled manual and managerial employment, 1964–68*

involved, we see a similar pattern of change; in spite of the
shrinkage in total employment in manufacturing industry, the
absolute total of manufacturing employment in these two
occupational categories has increased. This pattern is shown in
Table 7.1. This data only covers a period of four years; but when,
in following sections, we look at data extending over a longer
period we will see the same pattern – a general 'improvement' in
the quality of jobs over time.[6] What, therefore, was wrong with
the prediction, based on the principle of the division of labour,
that jobs would be degraded?

   To understand this, we must consider the peculiarly static view
of the relationship between technology and the division of labour
held by both Smith and Babbage. The division of labour was
aimed at improving the efficiency of performance of a sequence of
tasks which together produce the finished article. Both Smith and
Babbage talk as if the various tasks are given, as if they necessarily
existed before the innovation of divided production. Did the

TABLE 7.1 *Absolute change in skilled manual and managerial employment in the United Kingdom, 1964–8*

	Managerial, etc.	Skilled
1964	1923 551	2 661 900
1968	2 095 220	2 551 120
1968 − 1964	171 669	−110 780

$$\text{Slope } 1964 \rightarrow 1968 = \frac{\text{managerial workers in } 1968{-}1964}{\text{skilled workers in } 1968{-}1964}$$

$$= \frac{171\,669}{-110\,780}$$

$$= -1.55$$

individual undivided or autonomous pin-smith (if he ever existed, which is certainly open to doubt) carry out the entire sequence of operations described by Babbage? He may have done, but in all probability he did not; possibly he used a different and simpler manufacturing process, and produced a slightly different article. Yet in Babbage and Smith, at least when considering the division of labour directly, we find the implicit assumption of the immutability of the component tasks of a manufacturing process. When technological change is considered in this context, the change tends to be within a subdivided task, which certainly improves the speed and efficiency of performance of the task, but does not necessarily change its nature. Babbage classes the two major advantages of machines as 'the addition which they make to human power' and 'the economy they make of human time'; machines are in this view really no more than tools for increasing human potential – Babbage admits this explictly: 'The difference between a *tool* and a *machine* is not capable of very precise distinction . . . a tool is usually more *simple* than a machine; it is generally used with the hand, whilst a machine is generally moved with animal or steam power'. This, then, was the explicit ideology of the first industrial revolution: first, specialise to improve efficiency at a given task, then employ machines in order to make the worker at each task more productive. Certainly, this increased productivity might reduce overall employment in particular tasks, but the menu of tasks stayed the same. Though there might be, as it were, only one point-grinder where two went before, the point-grinder, machines notwithstanding, still ground points.

Neither writer, however, held rigidly to this static view of the structure of manufacturing processes outside the consideration of the division of labour; they both understood that technological change affects the menu of tasks as well as the efficiency of performance of individual tasks, even though neither of them integrated this insight properly into their views of industrial change. Indeed, Smith's very first mention of a technological development in *The Wealth of Nations* was of a feedback device which obviated the need for an attendant for a beam engine.[7] And Babbage (though this is not his primary purpose in the passage from which we shall quote) provides a very early description of how a process of division of labour in combination with a technological innovation may entirely remove the need for human intervention in some category of tasks.

Babbage starts by describing how, thirty-five years previously, the French mathematician M. Prony had set about the compilation of a large table of logarithms. Prony started by dividing his workforce into three groups:

The duty of . . . ('the first section . . . five or six of the most eminent mathematicians in France') was to investigate, amongst the various analytical expressions which could be found for the same functions, that which was most readily adapted to simple numerical calculation by many individuals employed at the same time. This section had little or nothing to do with the actual numerical work. When its labours were concluded, the formulae of the use of which it had decided, were delivered to the second section. . . . This section consisted of seven or eight persons of considerable acquaintance with mathematics: and their duty was to convert into numbers the formulae put into their hands by the first section . . . to deliver out these formulae to the third section, and receive from them the finished calculation. . . . The members of [the third section], whose numbers varied from sixty to eighty, received certain numbers from the second section, and, using nothing more than simple addition and subtraction, they returned to that section the tables in a finished state . . . these persons were usually found more correct in their calculations, than those who possessed a more extensive knowledge of the task. (Babbage, *On the Economy of Machinery, etc.*, pp. 194–5)

So far we have a classic application of the division of labour, with 15 per cent of the workforce employed in a responsible and challenging activity, and the other 85 per cent employed, as in Adam Smith's words, on the principle of 'reducing every man's business to some one simple operation, and making this operation the sole employment of his life' – except that in this case their business consisted of two operations, addition and subtraction. At this stage of the process the overall quality of working life has been degraded – the lone mathematician compiling tables has a great deal of drudgery, but at least the satisfaction of directing his own activity and varying its rhythm, and while the division of labour lifts the drudgery from the shoulders of the 15 per cent minority, it removes the autonomy and the sense of the purpose of the activity from the 85 per cent majority.

But Babbage does not see the process as ending here. He suggests a further stage of development:

When it is stated that the tables thus composed occupy seventeen large folio volumes, some idea may be formed of the labour. From that part executed by the third class, which might be termed mechanical, requiring the least knowledge and by far the greatest exertions, the first part were entirely exempt. . . . But when the *completion of a calculating engine shall have produced a substitute for the whole of the third section of computers*, the attention of the analysts will naturally be directed to simplifying its application, by a new discussion of the methods of converting analytical formulae into numbers. (Babbage, *On the Economy of Machinery, etc.*, p. 195, my emphasis.)

Elsewhere he proposes a device whereby the calculating engine would automatically set type for printing the tables, obviating in the process the need for proof reading. Whereas Prony's application of the division of labour to the problem inevitably reduces job satisfaction for all but a small minority, Babbage's proposed combination of organisational change and technological development has the effect of improving the quality of working life by removing the necessity for the boring repetition of simple tasks, and reserving only administration and problem-solving as human tasks. Just as Prony's process is a good example of the sorts of changes brought about by the first industrial revolution – the potentiation of human labour – so Babbage's is a fine premonition of (in the language of Vonnegut's *Player Piano*) the 'second industrial revolution' – the abolition of drudgery.

We must state our argument carefully. We are saying that the prediction of the progressive degradation of the quality of working life through the division of labour breaks down because it embodies two false assumptions; it assumes that the set of individual tasks which constitute a manufacturing process remains constant over time, irrespective of technological change; and it assumes that any technological change merely affects the efficiency of human performance of these individual tasks, and not the nature of the tasks. Now, certainly, if we allow these two assumptions, and consider only organisational change through the division of labour without technical development, then job degradation is a *necessary* outcome of any rational (in the special sense), capitalist management. But, if we allow organisational change in concert with technological development, job degradation, while still possible, is certainly not necessary; in the example we have considered, the change from a lone mathematician calculating tables single-handedly and with his own hands, to a platoon of numerical analysts and computer programmers devising algorithms for a mechanical calculator – incidentally, a remarkable vision for 1832 – can only be considered job enhancement. So we have an obvious conclusion; specialisation, where the most boring and repetitive specialities can be completely mechanised, does not necessarily imply job degradation – probably the opposite.[8]

However, this does not bring us immediately to a conclusion. So far, we have merely shown that the proportion of satisfactory to unsatisfactory jobs has no necessary tendency to decline over time; our naive prediction is still that the absolute number of satisfactory jobs should decline because of the productivity gains from specialisation and mechanisation – a prediction which is contradicted by our empirical findings. The prediction breaks down when applied to Babbage's scheme for calculating logarithms because it does not allow for the possibility of an extension in the market due to the reduced production costs; with a sufficiently elastic demand curve, if the increase in demand for the product due to the lowering of its price is large enough, an increase of productivity may lead to an increase in employment. And, similarly, it looks rather as if Braverman's thesis would not hold true when tested against Britain in the mid-1960s. So, just as there is no *necessary* reduction in the proportion of employment in satisfactory jobs in manufacturing industry with increasing productivity, so is there no *necessary* reduction in the absolute numbers in such employment.

This is such an important point that we should pause here to consider it. By job improvement we mean improving the extent of job satisfaction while maintaining the number of jobs. Now, in the illustrative single industry case we have been considering, we see that technologies adopted because of the improvements they bring in manpower productivity may result in better jobs, and that, depending on the shape of the demand curve for the product, they may also maintain or even increase the absolute number of jobs. We can extend this to include more than one industry; even if the innovating industry faces an inelastic demand curve, if other industries have growing markets and adequate scope for employment, jobs may still be improved. If, on the other hand, markets are not on the whole expanding, Braverman's thesis must necessarily hold good. What we are saying here is certainly not original, but it is of great importance; economic growth is a necessary condition for job improvement. Certainly, this enters the argument at a very superficial and simplified level, but the same lesson will nevertheless hold however thoroughly we investigate – indeed, we are arguing at this level precisely because it does seem to provide an adequate basis for a generalisation. At a given stable level of production, the only technological or organisational changes that will be voluntarily adopted are those which reduce costs, and by the same token, degrade labour; within the present economic system, the quality of working life may only be improved under conditions of economic growth. And we should add that though economic growth is necessary for improvement of jobs, it is not sufficient: we can easily imagine conditions of growth coincident with job degradation.

The explanation we have entered so far is essentially a technical one. Newly emergent technologies, together with new opportunities for industrial organisation and economic growth, combine to require a more highly skilled occupational profile – the pattern of change is the result of a 'pull' from some objective technical forces. But this ignores the possible impact of cultural change; in addition to technological 'pull' as an explanation for the increased numbers of skilled workers, we can also see the possibility of a cultural 'push'. As workers become richer, and as the alternatives to paid employment become less unpalatable, their expectations and aspirations will inevitably change. Jobs which were hitherto acceptable become unacceptable, or in a less extreme form, jobs which were previously carried out efficiently are carried out less efficiently; time and materials wastage, absenteeism and job turnover, all increase. In order to counter these tendencies, industrial managements may be *forced* to develop new technologies and organisational patterns; the 'advantage' to the capitalist in the new methods may not be in any inherent superiority of the new technique over the old, but rather, in its suitability for the newly-emerged requirements of the workforce. In fact, these two types of change will tend to go hand in hand, the new technologies and organisations and the new standards of expectation develop interactively. So our preliminary view of the reasons for the apparent net improvement in the quality of working life during the 1960s combine strands of two of the three types of explanation for increase in the number of service jobs outlined at the end of Chapter 5; in part the apparent increase in managerial and similar jobs is an aspect of the increasingly-technical nature of production processes – but we must not forget that the inherent desirability of such jobs may lead to some essentially cosmetic changes in job organisation and nomenclature. But before going any further in drawing conclusions we must look a little more widely at the pattern of change of occupations since 1961.

3 Occupational Change since 1961

The Department of Industry statistics used in the previous section cover the whole of manufacturing industry for only the five-year period 1964 to 1968; similar data is available for metal-using industries up to 1975 – see Figure 7.4. It shows us the same pattern; for every per cent reduction in skilled manual employment there was a 2.1 per cent increase in managerial employment. The data however cover only a quarter of the total workforce; for more general information we have to look to the

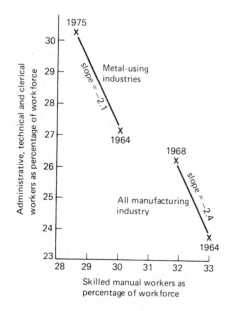

FIGURE 7.4 *Change in skilled manual and managerial employment in the United Kingdom, 1964–75 (proportions)*

information on occupation skill and status in the Population Census.

The Social Class categories used in the U.K. Census are somewhat confusing. They attempt to catch in one classification two almost orthogonal dimensions of social position – the level of skill or education requisite to a particular occupation, and the position in a hierarchy of authority in the employing organisation – see Table 7.2. Each occupational classification will have a basic level of skill attached to it, normally the level attributed to the 'other employees', and this basic level is

TABLE 7.2 *Two dimensions of social position in 'Social Class' in the United Kingdom*

Dimension 1 Requisite level of skill				
I Higher professional	II Lower professional	III Skilled, manual or non-manual	IV Semi-skilled	V Unskilled

Dimension 2 Hierarchical status			
Self-employed	Managers	Foremen	Other employees

modified by the individual's status to give his social class. So we can consider Table 7.3 for the occupational order 'Farmers, Foresters, Fishermen'. The 'basic level of skill' for each of these occupations except for farmers is IV, and Social Class is determined as this basic level modified by status, so that a farm-worker who has the status of manager falls into the Social Class II (lower professional). The reasons for these definitions are usually

TABLE 7.3 *Social class determined by occupational status*

	Self- employed	Managers	Foremen	Other employees
Fishermen	IV	IIIM	IIIM	IV
Farmers, etc.	II	II	–	–
Agricultural workers, n.e.c.	II	II	IIIM	IV
Agricultural machine drivers	II	II	IIIM	IV
Gardeners, etc	IV	IIIM	IIIM	IV
Foresters, etc.	II	II	IIIM	IV

quite clear, and the basic principles underlying them are carefully established in the relevant edition of *A Classification of Occupations*.

Nevertheless, for our purposes, this combination of two dimensions may be misleading; we wish to detect changes in numbers of skilled jobs *independent* of changes of hierarchical status. If we were to use the conventional five-fold Social Class as our indicator we could never be certain whether differences over time related to skill levels or status changes. We can see that, for example, a raising of status for an agricultural worker from 'other employees' to 'foremen' would also imply a raised social class from IV to III M, without any *necessary* change in skill, education or training. Our concern in this chapter is to investigate changes between relatively skilled and unskilled occupations; 'social class' is unsuitable because it does not allow us to estimate the proportion of change due to status transitions. This problem is not, however, insurmountable; we can apply a simple technique to break 'social class' into its two component dimensions. First, we take 'the social class' attribution of the lowest status for each occupation as an indicator for that occupation's 'basic level of skill' so that, in Table 7.3, all the occupations other than 'Farmers, etc.' have skill-level IV, and farmers have skill-level II. Then we add the information from the Occupation and Status tables in the Census, so that for each occupational order we have a two-dimensional tabulation of numbers in each occupational skill level at each status level. This is clearly an advantage over using 'social class' for our purposes; certainly, we are now underestimating skill-levels, instead of overestimating, since this procedure effectively assumes that no extra skills are implied by a rise in status. The separate estimate of status changes allows us, however, to put an upper limit on the extent of this under-estimation.

We will use here a rather cut-down version of this two-dimensional classification, aggregating the two professional skill levels (I and II) and concentrating the 'self-employed', 'managerial' and 'foreman' statuses into a single superordinate category, putting all other categories of employment into a second category. This enables us to get a picture of change in occupational distribution of the whole workforce over the decade between 1961 and 1971 – see Figure 7.5.

It will be helpful to start by considering the change in each of the occupational sectors individually. Primary occupational employment has fallen by more than one-third over this period; it is however noticeable that the decline was disproportionately among skilled and semi-skilled workers of subordinate status. Apparently the absolute total in skilled primary occupations, and in superordinate positions, hardly declined at all, so that the proportion in high skill and status occupations within the

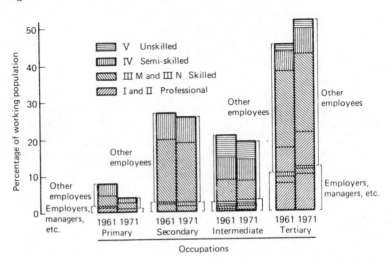

FIGURE 7.5   *Occupation, skill and status in the United Kingdom, for 1961 and 1971*

primary sector appears to have risen. This is, however, in part a result of a reclassification of underground workers in coalmines. Within the sector, the most striking trend is the decline in hired farm labour. Secondary occupations have again declined slightly in total, with a small increase in the proportion of semi-skilled workers to skilled, and again a small rise in the proportion of jobs with superordinate status. The proportion of the working population in the intermediate occupational sector fell by about 2 per cent; this is very largely accounted for by the reduction in the number of unskilled workers employed in manufacturing industry, though the fall in the numbers of skilled intermediate workers reflects the decline in the public transport system. Here again we see a rise in the number in superordinate occupations. In all, the primary, secondary and intermediate occupational sectors show a net loss of slightly more than 6 per cent of the working population, and the tertiary sector gains by this amount. The most marked change within the tertiary sector is in the category of professional jobs, the increase in which amounts to only slightly less than 5 per cent of the working population. The number of superordinate status jobs also increased by almost 2 per cent. Looking at the sectors individually, we see, as expected, a trend towards tertiary occupations, towards professional job categories and, perhaps less expectedly, towards more superordinate jobs. Does this add up to an overall improvement in jobs?

The data certainly do seem to be consistent with an overall improvement of jobs over the period. The proportion of the working population in professional jobs has increased by 4.2 per cent, and contrary to Braverman's 'polarisation' thesis, the rise in the professional category is not compensated for by a fall exclusively among skilled workers. In terms of our discussion in the previous section, the cross-time gradient of change in professional and skilled occupations is −3.2 per cent; that is, assuming constant employment, for every skilled manual or non-manual job lost, there were 3.2 new professional jobs. The proportion of total employment in unskilled jobs has risen, but only by one-tenth of one per cent; while the proportion in semi-skilled jobs is reduced by 2.5 per cent. In 1971, 21 per cent of the working population were in professional occupations (as against 16.8 per cent of the working population in 1961) and 48.5 per cent were in skilled occupations. In addition, the proportion of workers of superordinate status increased from 17.1 per cent to 19.5 per cent. By inference, therefore, working groups have become smaller, and so perhaps workers became on average closer to their immediate level of supervision.

These are, of course, the crudest possible indicators of the satisfaction derived from jobs. They measure merely the external attributes that place the limits on the possible intrinsic satisfactions of jobs. One particular worry is that the categories may have changed their meaning over the decade; we attach skill levels to individual occupations, and the content of these occupations may change over time so that the requisite level of training declines; though working groups have got smaller, their responsiveness to the suggestions and requirements of the individual worker may still have declined. The existence of an active trades union movement may result in the disguise of real processes of change by insisting on the maintenance of occupational or status categories over time.

The Census classification system is sensitive, to some extent at least, to such changes in the content of occupations. The 1971 *Classification of Occupations* lists some sixty-five alterations –

changes to the definitions of approximately one-quarter of the full list – to the classification since the 1961 Census, so that, for example, 'Engineers' (so described) who in 1961 were classed as skilled, had by 1971 been absorbed in the occupation of 'Machine tool operator' and classed as semi-skilled, restaurateurs rose from IV to III and chimneysweeps sank from IV to V.

The issues involved in a comparison of the subjective effects of changes in job content over time are really much too complex to be discussed here. Nevertheless, these two categories of skill and status distributions that we have discussed must count for something in the determination of the quality of working life, and so to the extent that we do consider the Census data as giving reliable estimates of these categories, and to the extent that the categories can be considered valid indicators, it would seem reasonable to conclude that over the period 1961 – 71, there was at least no decline in the quality of working life, and possibly some improvement. But, and this is the crunch, the 'sixties was a decade of relatively fast economic growth. Can we expect that the future growth rate will be sufficient to support full employment?

4 Job Design and Economic Growth

We started this chapter by considering two quotations from the 1950s which forecast the *total* automation of manufacturing industry. That automation has not yet happened, but the fact that it has been falsely predicted before is not a valid ground for rejecting any such prediction now. We can see a new sort of technical change. In the past technical advance in the manufacturing process took the form of specific machinery, either for potentiating workers (such advances are really improvements in tools) or of replacing particular human functions in the production of some particular good; technical change in the future seems likely to be not specific but generalised. Industrial robots will be designed not to carry out particular tasks but rather to learn to carry out any task just as a human worker does, a generalised technology for replacing the process worker in manufacturing production. Process manpower replacement by industrial robots would cause very fast rates of increase in manpower productivity.

The conventional view, as expressed in this chapter, is that relatively fast growth in productivity in some industries may perhaps displace some manpower, but over time this excess manpower is mopped up by new industries or by industries with slower growth in productivity. Manpower productivity in the manufacturing sector grew during the 1960s at an annual rate of about 3.5 per cent. G.N.P. rose slightly more slowly, but there was a net increase of employment enabled by transfers into lower productivity service industries. Our argument in the previous chapter suggested that the services cannot be expected to grow further – so they cannot be relied upon to soak up future employment. In the absence of a sink for displaced labour, and in order to maintain employment levels, consumption together with exports must rise in line with productivity; any future 3.5 per cent growth in manufacturing productivity must be matched by a similar rise in G.N.P. if it is not to cause unemployment. Can we expect to be able to match future productivity growth with G.N.P. growth in this way?

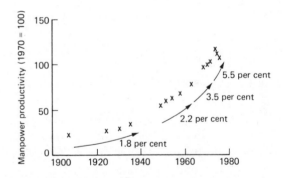

FIGURE 7.6   *Productivity growth in U.K. manufacturing industry, 1907–75*

It seems that the rate of growth in manufacturing manpower productivity in the United Kingdom has been growing continuously during this century – see Figure 7.6. In the years between the two world wars manpower productivity grew at perhaps 1.8 per cent per year. The rate of growth accelerated during the 1950s to about 2.2 per cent per year, to about 3.5 per cent during the 1960s, and to more than 5 per cent in the early part of this decade. Now even 3.5 per cent growth is a startlingly rapid rate – it means that the 1970 level of productivity would be doubled by 1990; and to maintain employment G.N.P. would also have to double. The rate of growth between 1970 and 1973, if it were to be resumed, would lead to a doubling of productivity by 1985, and a quadrupling by the year 2000 – see Figure 7.7.

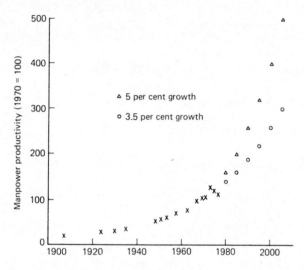

FIGURE 7.7   *Two estimates of manpower productivity growth, 1975–2005*

And given that the rate of productivity growth shows a broadly accelerating trend throughout the century, we might expect even faster rates of growth. We may be able to achieve quite significant rates of economic growth in the coming decades; we might even be able to maintain such growth rates for a longer period. But we certainly cannot expect to *increase* the rate of growth indefinitely. So if the rate of productivity growth continues to accelerate as it has done throughout this century, we can look forward in the long term only to a steady reduction in opportunities for work.

White-collar jobs in manufacturing industry have been increasing steadily throughout this century (see Figure 7.8) and since G.N.P. growth has not fallen behind productivity, this has not led to any significant losses of jobs. But the future may well be rather different. If changes in production technology do lead to a continuing trend of accelerating productivity growth – if, as seems likely, a large proportion of manufacturing industry does become very highly automated – the proportion of the workforce in such jobs will increase dramatically. The absolute number of white-collar workers may not grow very significantly, but they would constitute a rapidly increasing proportion of the total workforce. Many more of the available jobs would be non-manual – but there would be many fewer jobs.

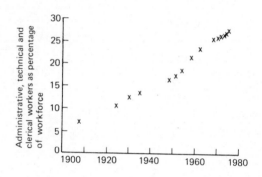

FIGURE 7.8 *Growth of tertiary occupational employment in U.K. manufacturing industry, 1907–75*

It has not happened before; but we are facing a new sort of technical change. In Chapter 3 we quoted Vonnegut's fictional description of the taping of Rudi Herz by the industrial robot.

> . . . this little loop in the box . . . here was Rudi as Rudi had been to his machine that afternoon – Rudi the turner on of power, the setter of speeds, the controller of the cutting tool. This was the essence of Rudi as far as the machine was concerned, as far as the economy was concerned. . . . The tape was the essence distilled from the small polite man with the big hands, and black fingernails. . . . (Vonnegut, *Player Piano*, p. 11)

Now consider the following:

> The welder at General Motors who takes a robotic welding device and guides its probes through the welding procedures of

a car body is on the one hand building skill into the machine, and deskilling himself on the other. The accumulation of years of welding experience is absorbed by the robot's self-programming system and will never be forgotten. (Cooley, pp. 74–5)[9]

Vonnegut's example was science fiction. Cooley's is in use today in Detroit. Certainly the general introduction of such machines is some way off: there is at the moment no generalised industrial robotics technology, but left to itself it certainly will come, in ten years or twenty. The potential for the increase of manpower productivity must by far outrun the potential for sustained economic growth in the developed world. The further we look into the future, the more likely a high and sustained rate of technological unemployment becomes.

CHAPTER EIGHT

CONCLUSION: A CHOICE OF FUTURES

1 Findings So Far

To pull together the threads of the argument, we might first of all summarise the discussion in the foregoing chapters. In Chapter 1 we considered the long pedigree of the improvement ideology – a history of opposition of social values to economic ones – which places the present controversy about an end to growth as merely a contemporary restatement of a traditional view. This raises a question, which forms the subject of the book: does the goal of improvement have some special relevance for Britain in the mid-1970s? Chapter 2 discusses the work of four contemporary writers who do feel the 'new theme' to be of particular relevance; we identify six principles which they hold to some extent in common – the emergence of new politically-relevant class cleavages, the increased importance of technocratic planning, an increasing role and scope for education, an increasingly non-material consumption pattern, higher expectations for the quality of working life, and an increasing flexibility in the design and scale of organisations. Underlying these is the broader concept that, for the developed world, historical economic expansion and present wealth imply a future in which growth of personal material consumption is of decreasing significance. The argument developed in the book is precisely that this broad concept is, though attractive as a statement of a social ideal, misplaced in any discussion of immediate economic policy, for growth in material prosperity has functions other than simply the satisfaction of material needs.

In Chapter 3, we make a first attempt to demonstrate this, by discussing two fictional accounts, one of a society based on the principle of social improvement, the other on the primacy of material consumption, both written by proponents of the improvement ideology, the former as exhortation, the latter as awful warning. But on reflection the message is not so very clear – on the one hand the ideal society does not seem to be a feasible aspiration for a developed Western state, since its pattern of development has been quite different, and on the other, if considered honestly, the dystopia does present some considerable advantages, at least in the short-term. Though it caters poorly for their spiritual values, its inhabitants are at least adequately fed and housed; for the presently developed world, economic growth does at least contain the possibility for alleviating the considerable poverty remaining within it; growth does seem to enable the continuation of political stability within a democratic form of government; growth might even enable us to help the less-developed world. The adoption of a policy of 'zero economic growth' would, it is suggested, hinder each of these goals.

But this anecdotal level of argument is not sufficient for an adequate demonstration; the remainder of the book is more specifically focused on two issues which are critical to the improvement thesis – the pattern of material consumption, which we investigate through the 'service economy' thesis, and the question of the 'improvement' of jobs. In Chapter 4, we consider the pattern of sectoral employment in Britain; we find that employment in primary industry falls over time, secondary industry at first rises and then falls, tertiary 'service' employment rises continuously. In fact, the evidence emboldens us to generalise a quite determinist sequence of development for employment sectors; up to a certain level of national product per head – around £900 in 1970 – the proportion of employment in manufacturing industry rises, and beyond that point it falls; at least, that was what happened in the O.E.C.D. between 1960 and 1974.

Proponents of the service economy, however, go on from observing the proportion of employment in the 'service' sector to assuming that an increased proportion of individual consumption consists of relatively non-material services which cater for the non-material needs which, they assert, come with increasing wealth. In Chapter 5, where we actually examine consumption patterns, we find that with the exception of medicine and education, the consumption of services in Britain has actually decreased considerably as a proportion of total consumption over the last twenty years. Though a new category of needs, corresponding to post-industrial demands for more recreational and other personal products, does emerge, these are met not by services but by goods. Precisely, we see a process of substitution; services which were previously provided from outside the household are increasingly replaced by production within the household using goods, essentially capital goods, acquired from manufacturing industry. The reason for this change is quite clear. New needs do arise with increased wealth, as do higher aspirations for occupational status. With the new spread of wealth in developed societies the demand for 'post-industrial' products rises, while the supply of labour available for their provision in the traditional labour-intensive, and in some ways personally demeaning, manner decreases; technological developments, however, enable provision on a much more capital-intensive basis, and self-served, rather than reliant on the service sector. In the past, education and medicine have been largely immune to this trend, both because of the conservatism of their suppliers and consumers, and because of the inherent technological problems: this is not likely to be the case in future.

So why the increase in service employment? In Chapters 5 and 6, we show that it comes largely from two sources. The first, in accordance with the service economy thesis, is the expansion of employment in medicine and education; but these, it is argued, will not grow as fast in the future, and may indeed contract as the 'self-service economy' expands to contain them. The other source, and this would seem to be a continuing trend, is the growth in those service industries (distribution, banking, insurance, finance) which have to do essentially with the system of material goods and their ownership, and those service occupations (managers, technologists and other professionals) whose activities aid the improvement of the efficiency of the system of material production. The growth of the service *employment* sector in the future is quite irrelevant to the behaviour of the service-consuming economy.

This is a fundamentally important observation. The 'goods to services' hypothesis is crucial to the improvement theorists' position. The post-industrial society can move from an 'econo-mising' basis for decision-making to a 'sociologising' basis; can move from the capitalist ethic to a 'communal' one simply because, as Bell asserts, 'the consumer-oriented, free-enterprise society no longer satisfies the citizenry'; sated with the possession of material goods, the post-industrial citizenry turns to non-material social values. We have demonstrated that the citizenry is by no means sated with material goods. It will, on the contrary, continue to demand more. The import of this argument is that the increase in consumption of consumer durables is not a flippancy, as Galbraith asserts, nor is it irrelevant to social improvement, as Dahrendorf implies. It is, in fact, either the substance or the manifestation of a social revolution – the change from a society of masters and servants both in personal consumption and in the manner of provision of that consumption, to a society of consumers, still unequal in the quantity of consumption perhaps, but increasingly equal in the way in which that consumption is provided.

The growth of provision of material goods is thus instrumental to a most significant social transformation – the democratisation of the means of provision for final consumption, as well as its distribution. In Chapter 7, we discuss another important benefit of economic growth. One shared aim of the improvement theorists is the improvement of the quality of working life; we argue that within the current framework of economic activity in Britain, jobs may only be improved on aggregate under conditions of economic growth. Technical developments must continuously improve manpower productivity; jobs are indeed likely to get more technically demanding, and hence possibly more rewarding, but if productivity rises without economic growth, total employment must inevitably fall. If the managers of manufacturing industry are to follow an economic rationality, and with our present economic structure as with any politically feasible alternative there is no other rationality for them to follow, they will adopt innovations in manufacturing technology as they occur. So, for Britain, assuming the continuation of a mixed economy, the cessation of economic growth would be inconsistent with the goal of improving jobs whilst maintaining their total numbers. And while readers of this book might argue that the possession of a paid job is not an absolute prerequisite for a good life, nevertheless, considering the sanctions currently enforced against those without jobs, and the political consensus on the desirability of full employment, the very unanimity of which implies its basis in more than economic motives, they must certainly consider that possession of a satisfying job is at least a short-term goal of a very large majority of the population.

2   A View of the Future

This argument is not merely an historical description, it contains
a prediction, though not an unconditional prediction; we make it
while reserving two classes of assumption. First, the compass of
the discussion is limited: we assume that there will be no radical
change in our geographical and environmental circumstances, in
geopolitics and in the international economic system, such as to
impose an exogenous check on long-term economic growth.
Second, and we shall return to this in the following section, we
assume that no public policies are adopted with the intention of
redirecting the trends we have observed. Given these assumptions, we have a clear view of the future, a view radically different
to those of the four theorists we have been considering.

In explaining this view, we might start with the accepted
conservative account of economic development which we discussed at the beginning of Chapter 1. Rostow's account of
sectoral development is that at the early stage of civilisation, with
rudimentary agricultural techniques, the majority of any population must work on the land; as techniques and productivity
improve, they are not so constrained and may move on to
different categories of production – secondary and then tertiary.
Rostow asks where we go from the stage of high consumption of
material goods; Bell answers that we pass on to the next category
of consumption, the consumption of services; Dahrendorf, similarly though in different terms, that we pass to the public
provision of non-material products, education and leisure activities; Schumacher, that we turn our attention to social and
spiritual values. Galbraith, rather differently, sees the trend as
ever-increasing material consumption, but only as a result of the
machinations of the great post-capitalist corporations of the
'planning system' for whom economic growth is a requisite of
survival. Once these corporations are controlled, then the
pattern of development may be trimmed to the public purpose,
which is assuredly not the continued growth in consumption of
material goods. The view of the future of employment for all
these writers is simply a continuation of Rostow's drift through
sectors classified by the nature of their final product; they see
post-industrial employment in a humanised form of manufactur-

ing industry and increasingly in tertiary service employment.

Our argument is that this view results from a confusion between employment and consumption patterns. Certainly post-industrial values tend towards the tertiary patterns of *consumption*, in the sense of their being more abstract, largely recreational or intellectual. But this does not mean that there is any necessary growth of tertiary *employment* on an equivalent scale. To put it crudely, if we want more food we manufacture more fertiliser and more tractors, we do not (though we could) employ more farmers. Meeting these more abstract tertiary needs does not necessarily require increased employment in service industries, and if the trends of the last few decades continue, future growth in tertiary needs will be met by increased production by manufacturing industry. The secondary sector produces capital items for the provision of final consumption; if final consumption becomes more capital intensive, the sector producing capital goods becomes increasingly important, and furthermore, since the labour used in the production of final tertiary product is increasingly 'direct' – that is, supplied by the final consumer – so we expect a progressive concentration of the paid labour force, either in manufacturing industry, or in those tertiary industries or occupations which directly aid material production.

The original basis for social cooperation was the benefit to be drawn from it; the division of labour and the advantages of scale are the progenitors of complex social organisation. The needs of the community in ancient times required the cooperation of the members of the community; the provision for these needs required a great deal of interpersonal contact: society was a process whereby people did things for people. Distribution of responsibility was not always equable, the concept of personal property, and particularly of the ownership of the means of production, introduce a distortion; the allocation of responsibilities into roles of differing desirability, delvers and spinners and gentlefolk. It is argued, particularly by those of the same cast of mind as our improvement theorists, that the growth in the scale and complexity of modern industry, together with the power of organised labour, have rendered class cleavages based on the ownership of capital less relevant. Be that as it may, a new cleavage in the relations of production is emerging. Production increasingly takes place in two quite separate phases; the first phase taking place outside the household consisting of the production of capital goods – social cooperation in the intermediate production of things, which increasingly constitutes the whole of the conventional economic process; the second phase takes place within the household, and consists of the direct production of the items of final consumption by the consumers themselves, using capital goods acquired from the manufacturing system.

There may therefore be some paradoxical truth in the improvement theorists' notion that the age of economics is passing. We can see an almost cyclical progress. We can go back further than Rostow and consider a primeval stage zero, where the dominant human activities were hunting and gathering, requiring no social cooperation – a stage essentially prior to economics. We now foresee the beginning of a post-economic era in which the final phases of the production process are similarly non-economic – private, and independent of cooperation. Certainly cooperation is necessary in the earlier phase of intermediate production of capital goods, but as techniques of automation improve, involvement in this cooperative phase of manufacturing outside the household will increasingly become the privilege of an elite. This is the world described in *Player Piano* – the class cleavage between capitalists and workers virtually inverted into an aristocracy of professional workers supporting a totally alienated proletariat whose productive activities are completely confined within the household.

We can put the argument of the book rather more simply. The conventional view of the sequence of economic development seems to come from a rather naive psychological view of a hierarchy of needs in the manner of Maslow. It starts with a statement of needs, first for food, then for shelter – the categories of need are mapped on to particular products and production sectors, food on to agriculture and so on. This is already a sort of theoretical justification of the Engel's curves – the higher in the hierarchy of needs, the lower the income elasticity of demand for the particular good. Now add to Engel's Law capital investment and labour substituting technical change, and we have the traditional 'Stages of Growth' in its crude form (Figure 8.1): first the pre-industrial economy with an employment hump in agriculture, then industrial, with the hump in manufacturing

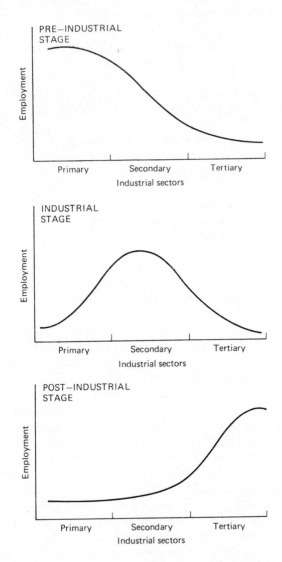

FIGURE 8.1 *Crude 'stages of growth' view of employment patterns*

industry, and then the 'post-industrial' with the hump in the tertiary sector.

The Service Economy thesis is really just the latest edition of the Stages of Growth approach. One of the implications of the objection to the thesis brought in this book is that the conventional sequence of stages is a misleading simplification of the process of economic development. There appear, from the foregoing argument, to be three different processes: (1) Change in the *production system*: technical and organisational change within industries – so that, for example, we see the growth of service occupational employment within manufacturing industry, partly as a result of inventions and investment, partly as a result of division of labour. (2) Changes in the *balance between industries* – so that for example a laundry (service) industry is progressively replaced by a washing machine (consumer durables) industry. (3) Changes in the *organisation of the household*, changes in the labour it provides to the money economy, and in the nature of the inputs to it from the money economy.

Simply, a given pattern of needs might be met by a number of different patterns of organisation of production and consumption. A model of development based on a one-dimensional classification of employment patterns, as is the Stages of Growth, must be misleading. We can get a better appreciation of the process of development with an only slightly more complicated model. We might start with two dimensions, occupation and industry. Table 8.1 is a reformulation of Table 6.8, taking account of the material output of 'producer services'.

The question we have tried to answer in this book is: 'What determines change in this matrix over time?' We have arrived at some sort of answer. First of all, in the east/west dimension we see two different components of change: an organisational component – 'the division of labour' – and a technical component – innovation and investment, which go together to change the distribution and the nature of jobs, the scale of output and the design of products. Similarly, movement in the north/south dimension has two components: organisation change – for instance, whether the provision is on a collective or an individual basis – the laundry versus washing machine example – and technical change, modifying the quantity of labour (skill level or time) input to production – the archetypal example here is the automatic 'player piano' – a technical innovation which enabled the direct substitution of a manufacturing industry product for a service industry product.

TABLE 8.1   *Distribution of occupations across industry in the United Kingdom, 1971*

		Occupation		
		Predominantly manual		Non-manual
		Primary Farmers, miners	*Secondary* Manufacturing processes, construction, transport	*Tertiary* Clerical, professional, administrative and sales
Predominantly material products	*Primary* Food, mined products	3.4	0.6	0.3
	Secondary Manufacturing production and ancillaries (distribution, financial and some* professional services)	0.6	34.5	27.8
Predominantly immaterial products	*Tertiary* Producing services (transport, some † professional services, other services and public administration)	0.4	7.8	24.6

* Accounting, legal services, research.
† Educational, medical, social, religious, cultural.

In terms of this analytical structure, the Service Economy thesis suggests a sort of undifferentiated drift to the south-east – see Figure 8.2(a). The Self-service Economy argument suggests that two separate trends are to be expected; an easterly trend in the occupational dimension, because of automation and division of labour, a trend towards more white collar employment; and a progressive concentration of employment in manufacturing industry – see Figure 8.2(b). These sum to a generally north-easterly drift – see Figure 8.2(c).

Associated with this drift comes a change in a third dimension. There is more and more capital investment in the home, an ever-increasing proportion of final consumption is produced in the

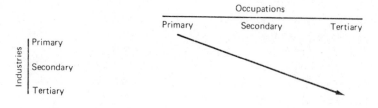

FIGURE 8.2 (a)   *'Service Economy' thesis*

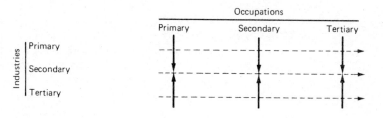

FIGURE 8.2 (b)   *'Self-service' Economy*

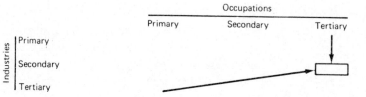

FIGURE 8.2 (c)   *Concentration of service occupations in manufacturing industry*

home, people's direct labour in the home becomes increasingly important as part of the total real product of the society.

Is the Self-service Economy a good place to be? There are two very serious problems. The first is unemployment. The trend is towards a concentration of employment in tertiary occupations – what proportion of the population can conceivably be employed here? The situation looks like being, to quote the 1950s American sociology, 'the professionalisation of everybody', only here with a crucial qualification – the professionalisation of everybody who isn't unemployed. The second problem is isolation. The household in the Self-service Economy is the kingpin of production and consumption. The current trend shows that as the self-service household becomes more self-sufficient, it also becomes more inward turning and less sociable. This may be acceptable in a society where the disciplines of sociability are imposed by the need to work in the money economy, but if there is no opportunity for work in the money economy, the members of the push-button self-servicing household may not be so happy.

By now it must be clear that the message of this book is that, of the two alternative fictional futures discussed in Chapter 3, the image in *Player Piano* is the more likely. We face a future in which an educated elite minority is employed in intrinsically rewarding technical tasks connected with the process of material production, and the majority is employed only in the undemanding manipulation of automated machinery for the satisfaction of their own needs, perhaps materially well provided for, but starved of rewarding occupation, mere machines for consumption. Is there anything we can do to avoid this society?

3 Three Strategies

To start with, we might try to stave off structural unemployment by subsidising underemployment in manufacturing industry. This is an approach favoured in the recent report to the O.E.C.D., *Towards Full Employment and Price Stability* (the McCracken Report):[1]

We have . . . been attracted by the schemes in a number of countries whereby, during a fixed period, private sector employers were paid a subsidy for employing new labour. (McCracken Report, para 349)

But this can, at best, only be a very temporary measure. It is liable to encourage inefficiency in the production process, and though it might bring gains in the form of reducing the necessary level of demand for any given level of employment, these are likely to be negated by the reduction in aggregate demand resulting from lost foreign markets. It may have a short-term appeal, but in the long-term it is likely to be self-defeating. A second strategy, also involving determined public intervention, would be the subsidy not of wasteful employment in manufacturing industry, but of further employment in tertiary industries. (This is also proposed in the McCracken Report, para. 347.) This, however, is again running against the economic tide; we saw in Chapter 5 that there is a trend away from the direct purchase of service. The current dissatisfaction with a high level of taxation to finance publicly subsidised service may be a manifestation of this phenomenon, and certainly public opposition to higher levels of spending on services seems likely to continue. And apart from this, there is also a question of equity to be faced: if our motive is *simply* to alleviate the problems of structural unemployment, to what extent can we justify additional expenditure on salaries in the service sector instead of an equivalent general increase in unemployment benefits?

Both of these strategies are essentially meliorative. They recognise the economic forces leading to a decline in the employment level, and attempt to oppose them artificially. The third strategy, instead of working against the trends, works with them. It has to do with the organisation of the household. What is it that makes activities in the household so unrewarding that employment in the money economy seems preferable to leisure? The answer concerns the assumptions underlying the design of the capital goods we install in households. It is assumed that work in the household is a marginal activity, to be undertaken in minimum time and with minimum effort. *Real* work, in the conventional view, is always to be undertaken outside the household: the home is merely a place for leisure. If the amount of time available is increased, of course, the design assumptions break down; we want to work in the money economy because households are designed specifically *not* to provide us with rewarding occupations.

Clearly, the third strategy is therefore to start to consider the redesign of the household, or rather to reconsider the social basis of final consumption, since the household may not be a suitable base for the sort of technical and organisational changes involved. Consider: if more time were available there would be no need to make the use of household capital so unrewarding. Take cooking for example: it is potentially the ultimate in non-alienated production. A pleasurable task in itself, it uses one's own capital and one's own labour for one's own consumption. So why stop at cooking? The level of investment in a middle-class kitchen could easily provide an adequate basic carpenter's or metalworking shop, or a pottery lathe and kiln. A very wide range of needs could be provided for in this manner, and a small commune or cooperative could provide an even wider range. My dinner parties involve the use of my labour and my household capital to provide for my friends and my own final consumption. Why should I not make furniture or crockery, or for that matter assemble more complicated goods from components manufac-tured in the money economy, on the same basis? As production in the money economy gets more efficient and simple capital goods get cheaper, the facilities for me to do this get ever more readily available. And if I had the opportunity to engage in this sort of production I might be considerably less unhappy about not having a job in the money economy.

This is, of course, an outlandish and outrageous suggestion. But consider it in a slightly more sober form; it suggests that we encourage the development, in the rich countries of the northern hemisphere, of a sort of dual economy. Whilst the first two strategies seek simply to counter the trend towards the self-service economy, this third strategy attempts to exploit its more positive features. We have already suggested that economic activity in the formal sector is increasingly concentrated in intermediate production – that is, in the production of consumer durables which are in essence capital goods – and that these capital goods are invested in the informal sector of the economy for the production of final commodities. The 'dual economy' strategy would not seek to discourage the continuing drive for efficiency, with accompanying unemployment, in the formal sector. Instead it would seek to improve the quality of both work and leisure in the informal sector; indeed, since in this sector production and consumption activities are based on the same social unit, the distinction between work and leisure might itself become less clear-cut. As a result of this strategy the complex of activities including recreation, education, housework and other production activities which might in the future be transferred to the informal sector, might become a viable alternative to employment in the formal sector.

This, finally, is the significance of the improvement theorists. Small is beautiful – but not uniquely so. Much of the future of small-scale production will be due to large-scale production that produces the cheap productive capital and materials. The improving societies that the improving authors discuss – the focus on the bettering of work and leisure and their integration, on education and recreation, on *social* values rather than *economic* ones – are in fact to be based on an efficient and growing material production. The focus of change is not on movement from the economic to the social; rather the boundary between the two is moving. To avoid the worst of the possible attributes of the coming self-service economy, we must not try to stave it off, but rather try to exploit its promise for the closer harmonisation of the social and the economic realm.

NOTES AND REFERENCES

Introduction

1. Ralf Dahrendorf, *The New Liberty* (London: Routledge and Kegan Paul, 1975).

2. G. K. Chesterton, *The Napoleon of Notting Hill* (London: John Lane, 1904).

3. John O'Hara, *Appointment in Samarra* (New York: Duell, 1934).

4. Daniel Bell, *The Coming of Post-Industrial Society* (London: Heinemann, 1974).

5. E. F. Schumacher, *Small is Beautiful* (London: Blond and Briggs, 1973).

6. J. K. Galbraith, *Economics and the Public Purpose* (London: Andre Deutsch, 1974).

7. The final quotation in this paragraph is taken from A. Etzioni, *The Active Society* (New York: Free Press, 1968) pp. 5–6. The full passage is as follows:

> In his pains to master his fate, man is reaching a new phase in which his ability to gain freedom, as well as his ability to subjugate others, is greatly extended. Both of these build on his increasing capacity to transform bonds rather than to accommodate to, or merely protest, the social pattern he encounters. The post-modern period will be marked, in addition to a continued increase in the potency of instruments available and an exponential growth of knowledge, by man's potential ability to control both. An active society, one which realises this potential, would differ from modern societies in this key way: It would be a society in charge of itself rather than unstructured or restructured to suit the logic of instruments and the interplay of forces they generate.

8. The conventional economic wisdom has been until very recently that on the whole advantages to scale are maintained in advanced economies. This position was stated by Bain in *Barriers to New Competition* (Harvard University Press, 1956) and recent

studies of plant economies in a very wide range of U.K. industries – C. Pratten, *Economics of Scale in Manufacturing Industry* (Cambridge University Press, 1971) – seemed to lead to the same conclusion. However, S. J. Prais in *The Evolution of Giant Firms in Britain* (London: NIESR, 1976) finds that in the U.K. economy as a whole over the last forty years, though plant sizes have risen somewhat, the *range* of sizes of plant has also risen considerably both in aggregate and within most individual industrial sectors. He concludes that 'considering manufacturing as a whole, or broad industrial groups such as engineering or food production . . . there is scope today for a wider absolute range of sizes than previously' (p. 59). He suggests that the explanation for the growth of sizes of *firms* must be sought for elsewhere than in technical advantages of scale in production. Prais (pp. 52–3) gives the following example of how advantages to scale may be decreased over time:

Up to the 1930s the application of electric power to a machine in a factory normally involved a vast mechanical link. The advent of electricity had permitted smaller factories to benefit from power driven machinery by installing their own electric motors; but motors were expensive, and within each factory there was to be found a central transmission shaft driven by that motor. Individual machines were driven by a leather belt from that shaft much as in earlier days when the central shaft was driven by steam or another source of power. A considerable overhead investment was therefore necessary before a plant could take advantage of electric power. Since that time the costs of electric motors have fallen to such an extent that today it is normal for each machine to be equipped with its individual small motor; the central transmission shaft has been abolished, with savings in energy transmission costs and benefits from more flexible plant-layouts. As Siemens had foreseen, in a remarkable passage written a hundred years ago, the development of electric power would 'in the course of time produce a revolution in our conditions of work in favour of small-scale industry'.

The impact of the reduction in the cost of capital goods over time on the organisation of production will emerge as an important theme in the later chapters of this book.

9. This is based on an analysis of the various systems described in Bernhard E. Nickel, *Bibliography of Unconventional Passenger Transport Systems* (Bruxelles: Union Nationale des Transports Publics, 1973).

10. This novel viewpoint is proposed by R. Dawkins in *The Selfish Gene* (Oxford University Press, 1976).

11. See, for example, D. Braybrooke and C. E. Lindblom, *A Strategy of Decision: Policy Evaluation as a Social Process* (New York: Free Press, 1963).

Chapter One

1. Ralf Dahrendorf, *The New Liberty*.

2. W. W. Rostow, *The Stages of Economic Growth: A Non-Communist Manifesto* (Cambridge University Press, 1960). The account in the following two paragraphs is a summary of pp. 6–16. Rostow may well have been an innovator in the formulation of 'stages of growth' theories, but he has certainly not been without imitators. Michael Marien, in *Societal Directions and Alternatives* (LaFayette, New York: Information for Policy Design, 1976) lists no less than 64 distinct 'stages' theories. The present author is forced to admit that it is partly knowledge of the volume of potential competition that leads him to insist that the self-service economy is not to be considered as a new developmental stage. However, see section 2 of the concluding chapter of this book.

3. Rostow, however, stresses that this is not a rigidly determined process – in this respect he carefully distinguishes the scope of his theory from that of Marx (*The Stages of Economic Growth*, p. 150).

4. Rostow identifies 'Buddenbrooks dynamics':

In Thomas Mann's novel of three generations, the first sought money; the second, born to money, sought social and civic position; the third, born to comfort and social prestige, looked to the life of music.

He is, however, very chary of 'an adventure in generalisation' on this basis, and only goes as far as asserting that:

> the implications of the baby boom along with the not wholly unrelated deficit in social overhead capital are likely to dominate the American economy over the next decade rather than the further diffusion of consumer durables. (pp. 11–12)

5. J. S. Mill, *Principles of Political Economy* (London: Longman, 1892). This edition (identical to the Sixth Edition) is the source for all the following quotations.

6. See Rostow, *The Stages of Economic Growth*, p. 68, and also the diagram facing page 1.

7. For evidence of this, consider:

> When a country has long possessed a large production, the rate of profit is habitually within, as it were, a handsbreadth of the minimum, and the country therefore on the very verge of the steady state. By this I do not mean that this state is likely in any of the great countries of Europe, to be soon actually reached, or that capital does not still yield a profit considerably greater than what is barely sufficient to induce the people of those countries to save and accumulate. My meaning is, that it would require but a short time to reduce profits to the minimum, if capital continued to increase at its present rate, and no circumstances having a tendency to raise the rate of profit occurred in the meantime. The expansion of capital would soon reach its ultimate boundary, if the boundary itself did not continually open and leave more space. . . . We may conclude . . . that improvements in production, and emigration of capital to the more fertile soils and unworked mines of the uninhabited or thinly populated parts of the globe, do not, as it appears to a superficial view, diminish the gross produce, and the demand for labour, but on the contrary, are what we chiefly have to depend on for increasing both, and are even the necessary conditions of any great or prolonged augmentation of either. Nor is it any exaggeration to say that within certain, and not very narrow, limits, the more capital a country like England expands in these two ways, the more she will have left. (Mill, *Political Economy*, pp. 443–51)

8. That is, Mill, *Political Economy*, chapters 4 and 5 of Book 4.

9. The author is not an expert on palaeoeconomics, and has thus been forced to rely very heavily on secondary sources in this section; many of the ideas, and some of the quotations, that follow come from M. Beer, *An Enquiry into Physiocracy* (London: Allen and Unwin, 1939) and B. Gordon, *Economics Before Adam Smith* (London: Macmillan, 1975).

10. Beer, *An Enquiry into Physiocracy*, p. 55.

11. Gordon, *Economics Before Adam Smith*, pp. 17–20 introduces this anonymous text as an example of Sophist economics, but stresses that its precise date and attribution are uncertain.

12. Lord Robbins, *An Essay on the Significance of Economic Science* (London: Macmillan, 1952).

13. E. F. Schumacher, *Small is Beautiful*, pp. 99–100.

14. R. Dahrendorf, *The New Liberty*, pp. 8–10.

15. To be fair, Schumacher does mention in the Epilogue to his book that there is a Christian tradition that corresponds to the Buddhist tradition cited in the body of the text.

Chapter Two

1. We must bear in mind that Dahrendorf, in *The New Liberty* (London: Routledge and Kegan Paul, 1975), clearly rejects any uncompromising zero-growth position:

> . . . we have to change . . . the subject of history if we want to solve the problems of the day in a liberal manner. Of course we need economic growth in order to cope with the problems of poverty and inequality, and even of pollution and food scarcity; but it must not and cannot remain the centre of our attention if we seek the new liberty. (Dahrendorf, *The New Liberty*, p. 10)

2. For a disenchanted analysis of the motives underlying *The Limits to Growth*, see R. Golub and J. Townsend, 'Malthus, Multinationals and the Club of Rome', *Social Studies of Science*, 7, 2 (June 1977).

3. D. Bell, *The Coming of Post-Industrial Society* (London: Heinemann, 1974). See table 1.1, p. 117.

4. 'A Remarkable Parallel' is the subtitle to chapter 7 in *The Stages of Economic Growth*, in which Rosow describes the similarity in the patterns of growth of the United States and the USSR.

5. Bell asks the question (pp. 456-66) but he does not actually answer it. He does go as far as to paraphrase Keynes' position as 'Basic needs are satiable and the possibility of abundance is real', and though Bell is careful not to tell us whether he agrees with the opinion he has stated on behalf of Keynes, the general tenor of the discussion on this page (456) is positive. However, by p. 467 the sense of the argument has shifted somewhat: 'In a technical sense, the elimination of scarcity means a situation of zero cost, and this is impossible. In sum the concept of the abolition of scarcity is an empirical absurdity'. Elsewhere it does become plain that Bell considers that in the future problems of material production will lose importance and problems of management and control will gain ('The New Scarcities', pp. 466-75); we are however still left with a series of somewhat contradictory statements throughout the book of his own opinion as to the end of material scarcity. Professor Bell's complex thought is sometimes difficult to master.

6. C. Clark, *The Conditions of Economic Progress* (London: Macmillan, 1940).

7. Details of this scheme are to be found in 'On the Probable Futurity of the Labouring Classes' in Mill, *Political Economy*, pp. 455-76.

8. S. M. Miller, in 'Notes on Neo-Capitalism', *Theory and Society*, 2, 1975, pp. 1-35, points out that the Roman Empire was dependent on literate Greek slaves for its smooth running; this putative knowledge elite would hardly be considered to hold political power in any of the normal senses of the word. They certainly had some potential for power, and had they organised themselves into a political faction they might have gained power, rather in the manner of Wells' airmen in *The Shape of Things to Come* – but that is a characteristic that applies equally to technocrats and coalminers.

9. The quotations in this section are taken from the U.K. edition of the book: J. K. Galbraith, *Economics and the Public Purpose* (London: Andre Deutsch, 1974) – abbreviated to *EPP*.

10. The brevity of the discussions of each of the books in this chapter inevitably leads to distortion. The distortion in this discussion of Schumacher's *Small is Beautiful* (London: Blond and

Briggs, 1973) is even more marked than elsewhere; fully half of Schumacher's book concerns the Third World, all of which discussion goes unmentioned here.

Chapter Three

1. Quotations are from Aldous Huxley, *Island* (London: Penguin, 1964).

2. Quotations are from K. Vonnegut, *Player Piano* (London: Panther, 1975).

3. Fred Hirsch, in his recent book *The Social Limits to Growth* (London: Routledge and Kegan Paul, 1977), argues that competition for more advantageous positions is a zero-sum game even under conditions of economic growth. The next section of this chapter will investigate his argument.

4. See, for example, H. Kahn, W. Brown, L. Martel, *The Next 200 Years* (New York: Morrow, 1976); C. Freeman, M. Jahoda (eds), *World Futures: The Great Debate* (London: Martin Robertson, 1978).

5. D. Meadows *et. al.*, *Limits to Growth* (New York: Universe Books, 1972).

6. See H. S. D. Cole *et. al.*, *Thinking About the Future* (London: Chatto and Windus, 1973).

7. An alternative arrangement is the current practice in Poland. There is still a market for privately owned historical works of art; the rights of ownership are however modified by a requirement that owners agree to public exhibition of works of art for up to six months of the year.

8. See L. Davis, *Design of Jobs* (London: Penguin, 1972), or L. Klein, *New Forms of Work Organisation* (Cambridge University Press, 1976).

Chapter Four

1. A. Smith, *The Wealth of Nations* (London: Methuen, 1961).

2. Table 4.1 involves some heroic assumptions about the continuity of categories and definitions, and each number in it is certainly open to question. The broad trends it shows do however seem to be the subject of agreement among economic historians, including the surprising constancy of the manufactur-

ing employment proportion through this period. The manufacturing estimates in this table (its sources are given, as are those of all the tables, in the next section – Tables and Figures: Sources and Comments) agree with those of Deane and Cole (P. Deane and W. A. Cole, *British Economic Growth 1688–1959* (Cambridge University Press, 1969) p. 144):

> In the first decade of the nineteenth century [the manufacturing group of industries] probably absorbed less than a quarter of the occupied population of Great Britain. By 1841 (perhaps by 1831) they had expanded their share to about a third, and from then until the First World War they grew, in numbers at any rate, more or less in step with the total British Labour force. They still claimed only a third of the labour force in 1911, but in 1921 their share reached 36 per cent, and in 1951, 39 per cent.

3. R. Heilbronner, *Business Civilisation in Decline* (London: Boyars, 1976) p. 65:

> The great sectoral transformation of our times . . . has not been so much a shift from industry to services as a shift from agriculture to service tasks.

4. Table 4.6 is also subject to considerable question. A research assistant who recompiled this table as a check found a very extensive set of divergences simply by taking estimates of the same year's employment from a different year's handbook. The trends described in the following paragraph however appeared unchanged in this new table, so while the data may be unreliable, the pattern they describe still seems to be the correct one.

5. We must be cautious in generalising from this model, which is after all merely a static lateral picture of the behaviour of *different* states at the *same* point in time. The data provide insufficient information to assume that the longitudinal picture, the dynamic behaviour of individual states over time, should follow this pattern of decreasing proportional employment in manufacturing having passed the 'post-industrial transition' of £900 per capita G.N.P. However the fact that Japan, which has passed this boundary, has had a decreasing employment in

manufacturing industry since 1973, may be an indication that the model is a reasonable dynamic description of this aspect of economic development.

Chapter Five

1. C. Northcote Parkinson, *Parkinson's Law* (London: Penguin, 1970).

2. A somewhat similar formulation is to be found in Scott Burns, *The Household Economy* (Boston: Beacon Press, 1976). Burns suggests that household investment in the United States has a higher real rate of return to the individual than any available alternative.

Chapter Six

1. These industries have been described as 'producer services': ' . . . services which business firms, non-profit institutions, and governments provide and usually sell to the producer rather than the consumer' – H. I. Greenberg, *Manpower and the Growth of Producer Services* (New York: Columbia, 1966) p. 1. Such services are distinct from the services provided by non-manual employees of manufacturing industries, which are discussed in the next section – but both have in common that they provide for the final consumption of goods.

2. Bell, *The Coming of Post-Industrial Society*, p. 15.

3. Table 6.8 is reformulated in Table 8.1 to take account of producer service activities.

4. R. Bacon and W. Eltis, *Britain's Economic Problem: Too Few Producers* (London: Macmillan, 1976).

5. Bacon and Eltis, *Britain's Economic Problem*, p. 11.

Chapter Seven

1. S. Lilley, *Automation and Social Progress* (London: Lawrence and Wishart, 1957).

2. P. Einzig, *The Economic Consequences of Automation* (London: Secker and Warburg, 1957).

3. H. Braverman, *Labour and Monopoly Capital* (New York: Monthly Review Press, 1974).

4. Charles Babbage is now chiefly remembered as the inventor of a mechanical forerunner of the computer. His father was a banker, which presumably explains his familiarity with the economics of his time. The book from which we quote here – *On the Economy of Machinery and Manufacturers* (London: Charles Knight, 1832), the quotations here being from the fourth edition, 1835 – arises, however, directly from his efforts to build his 'analytical engine'. He tells us in his Preface:

> The present volume may be considered as one of the consequences that have resulted from the Calculating Engine, the construction of which I have been so long superintending. Having been induced, during the last ten years, to visit a considerable number of workshops and factories, both in England and on the Continent, for the purpose of endeavouring to make myself acquainted with the various resources of mechanical art, I was insensibly led to apply to them those principles of generalisation to which my other pursuits had naturally given rise.

This early piece of spin-off from computer research provides a rather modern-sounding survey of the industrial economics of his time; his central theme is the impact of technology on the productive process and considers such issues as recycling of waste materials, the useful life of machinery and the promise of scientific ingenuity for solving future problems. He considers the exhaustion of the coal mines (p. 338) as well as the conventional economic issues of his time.

5. We see from Table 6.11 above that clerical employment in manufacturing industry stayed constant between 1961 and 1971 at 6 per cent of the workforce.

6. We must take a reservation: we cannot be certain that the apparent overall increase in skilled employment reflects any real change. The information on which we base our argument is not very reliable; it all comes from postal surveys which can only receive the most rudimentary of supervision. But this is the only aggregate data we have (or can reasonably expect), so we must make do with it; though we cannot estimate the size of errors, we can at least hope to spot systematic tendencies for inaccuracies. Starting with manual occupations, there is a natural tendency for

individuals to claim for themselves as high a status as possible, so we would expect that surveys such as the Census in which individuals are required to report on their own status will overestimate the numbers of skilled as against unskilled workers. Indeed, when we compare the Census estimates of numbers in skilled manual occupations with the National Insurance data presented in previous pages we do see a discrepancy; and to the extent that the National Insurance data is compiled from returns from manufacturing enterprises, which have no reason to exaggerate, we will inevitably have to conclude that the Census overestimates numbers in skilled manual jobs, rather than that the National Insurance data underestimates them. Similarly, in managerial, professional, and technical occupations, the Census estimates – particularly in the 1950s – are considerably higher than the National Insurance figures. This, however, seems to result from opposite tendencies, since the National Insurance information suffers from a systematic tendency to underestimate, due to National Insurance fraud, whereas the prevalence of national standards of status, or at least standards having meaning outside the firm, for these workers, would probably make self-reporting Census returns more reliable. As regards the data we have been discussing in this section, it is the result of a special survey, carried out under unusually strict supervision, and probably constitutes the best single source of aggregate data on the subject.

In addition, we must question how validly our information represents the changes we are interested in. Some recent writers – for example, M. Cooley, 'Contradictions of Science and Technology in the Productive Process', in H. and S. Rose (eds), *The Political Economy of Science* (London: Macmillan, 1976) and K. Kumar, 'The Industrial Societies and After', *Universities Quarterly*, 1975/6, p. 383 – have challenged the assumption that there has been any significant change in job content, arguing that the apparent changes reflect merely alterations of nomenclature. Certainly this may be true to some extent; much of the trend in skilled manual employment in the Census may be due to the renaming of jobs rather than their restructuring. But in the particular data we have been considering in this section, the criticism is invalid, since 'skilled jobs' are defined as those requiring an apprenticeship or other lengthy period of training.

Service occupational statistics may also be misleading in a similar manner, because changing styles of organisation may radically change the functions attached to particular professional or executive titles. We will be unable to make any generalisation on the aggregate data, but at least we will be able to see in detail the nominal pattern of change in these occupations.

To sum up, it is not claimed that the stock of jobs in manufacturing industry has actually improved over the brief period we have considered – but merely that it may have done. On the basis of the two errors we detect in the Smith–Babbage–Braverman theory – the mutability of the manufacturing process over time, and the possibility of elastic demand curves for the products of innovative industries – we can see that there is no *inevitable* tendency for the aggregate quality of jobs to decline with technical or organisational change. This tentative conclusion is sufficient to allow us to dismiss one of the three views on automation spelled out at the beginning of this chapter. However desirable may be the socialisation of capital for other reasons, it cannot be justified as a necessary condition for the improvement of the quality of working life. Such improvement is possible even without 'extra-economic' intervention in the capitalist system.

7.   In the first fire-engines (i.e., steam engines), a boy was constantly employed to open and shut alternatively the communication between the boiler and cylinder, according as the piston either ascended or descended. One of those boys, who loved to play with his companions, observed that, by tying a string from the handle of the valve which opened this communication to another part of the machine, the valve would open and shut without his assistance, and leave him at liberty to divert himself with his playfellows. (Smith, *The Wealth of Nations*, Vol. 1, pp. 13 and 14)

8. The argument as it stands makes the assumption that professional jobs in manufacturing industry are likely to be rewarding. This is by no means necessarily true; Mike Cooley has argued in a recent article – 'Contradictions of Science and Technology in the Productive Process' in H. and S. Rose (eds) *The Political Economy of Science* (London: Macmillan, 1976) – that just as technical innovation has in the past led to

deskilling of manual jobs, so present technical and organisational change lead to the deskilling of professional workers. He cites as an example the HARNESS computer package which reduces architects to the level of children playing with bricks. This observation (which he shares with Braverman) certainly seems valid; its implications are ignored in the following argument only for the purpose of showing that the prospects for employment are rather dismal in the longer term even when we make optimistic assumptions about the direct impact of change in manufacturing technology.

9. Cooley, 'Contradictions of Science and Technology in the Productive Process'.

Chapter Eight

1. P. McCracken *et al.*, *Towards Full Employment and Price Stability* (Paris: O.E.C.D., 1977).

THE TABLES AND FIGURES: SOURCES AND COMMENTS

TABLE 3.1   Source: *Family Expenditure Survey 1973*.

TABLE 4.1   Sources: *British Labour Statistics 1886–1968*, tables 102 and 103, *Census of Population 1971; Summary Tables*. For slightly different estimates, which nevertheless show the same trends, see Deane and Cole, *British Economic Growth*, table 31.

TABLE 4.2   Sources: as Table 4.1.

TABLE 4.3   Source: as Table 4.1.

TABLE 4.4   Source: *Census of Population 1971, Economic Activity* (10 per cent sample) table 22.

TABLE 4.5   Calculated from Table 4.4.

FIGURE 4.1   Source: B. R. Mitchell, *European Historical Statistics* (London: Macmillan, 1975) table c.1

TABLE 4.6   Source: O.E.C.D., *Labour Force Statistics*, 1960–74.

FIGURE 4.2   Constructed from Table 4.6.

TABLE 4.7   Sources: *British Labour Statistics 1886–1968*, table 135; and *Department of Employment Gazette*, June 1972 and April 1977.

TABLE 4.8   Sources: *British Labour Statistics 1886–1968*, table 108; and *British Labour Statistics Yearbook 1974*, table 105.

FIGURE 5.3   Sources: *Report of an Enquiry into Family Expenditure 1953–4*, and *Family Expenditure Survey* for 1961, 1966, 1971 and 1974. 'Services' include postage, telephone, telegrams, cinemas, theatres and other entertainments, licence and rents of radio and television, domestic help, hairdressing, repairs to footwear and other personal belongings, laundry and associated expenses, educational and training expenses, medical, dental and nursing fees, subscriptions and donations, hotel and holiday expenses. 'Transport' includes purchase and maintenance of motor vehicles, bus and railway fares, and other transport expenses such as prams and bicycles. 'Durables' include durable household goods such as televisions, radios (their purchase and repair), household furnishings and appliances, other goods such as books, toys, medicines, toilet requisites, and clothing and footwear. 'Alcohol etc.' includes both alcohol and tobacco. 'Food' includes meals eaten out of the home. 'Housing' includes both expenditure on rent,

TABLE A.1 *Average family expenditure in 1970 prices* (£)

	1954	1961	1966	1971	1974
Housing	2.95	3.81	4.72	5.38	6.00
Food	7.01	7.53	7.56	7.40	7.71
Alcohol, etc.	5.40	6.05	6.40	6.58	7.74
Transport	1.48	2.55	3.16	3.93	4.23
Services	1.99	2.35	2.51	2.68	3.03
Music	0.10	0.10	0.10	0.08	0.15

mortgages, etc., and on fuel, light and power. The data from which Figure 5.3 is constructed are shown in Table A.1.

TABLE 5.1   Sources: as for Figure 5.3.

TABLE 5.2   Sources: as for Figure 5.3. 'Transport Goods' here includes all expenditure on purchase, running and upkeep of private vehicles. 'Transport Services' comprises all bus and train fares.

FIGURE 5.4   Source: *Report of an Enquiry into Family Expenditures 1953–4.* Here 'Durables' exclude 'clothing' and 'other goods'. The data are given in Table A.2

FIGURE 5.5   Sources: *Report of an Enquiry into Family Expenditure 1953–4, Family Expenditure Survey 1974.* The data are given in Table A.3.

TABLE 5.3   Sources: as for Figure 5.3.

TABLE 5.4   Sources: as for Figure 5.3, the price indices are calculated from *British Labour Statistics 1886–1968*, tables 92 and 93, and the *Department of Employment Gazette*, taking 1954 as 100.

FIGURE 5.6   Sources: as for Figure 5.3, the price indices are calculated from *British Labour Statistics 1886–1968*, tables 92 and 93, and the *Department of Employment Gazette*. Taking 1954 as 100 the full set of price indices are given in Table A.4. These statistics should be treated with caution, since the basis on which the various price indices are calculated has changed several times over the period. Nevertheless, these changes are sufficiently small that certainly the larger relative changes – housing and services on one side, durables on the other – are reliably indicated. Using these indices we can recalculate the 1954 expenditure reflating each category by its *individual* price index to give an indication of the level of consumption, in 1974 terms, that it indicates. Summing the various expenditures for

TABLE A.2 Family expenditure in 1954

		Weekly budget of household (£)								
		9.04	14.61	22.73	26.00	31.85	39.92	54.78	74.80	130.10
Expenditure (£)	Food	3.40	5.81	9.50	9.69	11.22	12.02	16.41	18.34	21.83
	Durables	0.35	0.72	1.31	1.85	2.28	2.97	4.04	4.69	4.85
	Services	0.76	1.02	1.53	1.85	2.57	3.99	6.05	13.71	30.39
Expenditure as % of budget	Food	37.6	39.8	41.8	37.3	35.2	30.1	30.0	24.5	16.8
	Durables	3.9	4.9	5.8	7.1	7.2	7.4	7.4	6.3	3.7
	Services	7.7	7.0	6.7	7.1	8.1	10.0	11.0	18.3	23.4

TABLE A.3 Family expenditure in 1974

		Weekly budget of household (£)														
		14.04	14.74	18.93	23.62	27.55	30.83	35.31	36.59	41.98	45.68	52.01	59.32	65.63	77.59	101.86
Expenditure (£)	Food	4.57	4.42	5.79	7.16	8.08	8.84	9.77	9.75	11.49	11.93	12.87	14.10	14.81	16.60	19.01
	Durables	0.58	0.66	0.64	1.35	1.55	1.65	1.66	2.44	3.04	3.10	3.76	5.57	6.53	7.75	9.11
	Services	1.15	1.17	1.69	2.25	2.17	2.58	2.94	2.94	3.21	4.10	4.89	4.77	6.25	8.79	14.13
Expenditure as % of budget	Food	32.6	30.0	30.6	30.3	29.3	28.7	27.7	26.7	27.2	26.1	24.8	23.8	22.6	21.4	18.7
	Durables	4.1	4.5	3.4	5.7	5.6	5.4	4.3	6.7	7.2	6.8	7.2	9.4	10.0	10.0	8.9
	Services	8.2	7.9	8.9	9.5	7.9	8.4	8.3	8.0	7.7	9.0	9.4	8.0	9.5	11.33	13.9

TABLE A.4   *Relative growth of prices in the United Kingdom, 1954–74*

	Prices 1974 (1954 = 100)	Relative growth 1954–74 (All = 100)
Housing	359.2	134
Fuel	314.7	117
Food	289.7	108
Alcohol	200.1	74
Tobacco	209.0	78
Clothes	199.6	74
Durables	187.0	70
Other goods	277.0	103
Transport	269.4	101
Services	321.5	120
All	267.8	100

each income category, we get new 'real consumption' estimates for the size of the 1954 budgets. The net estimates for the three consumption categories we have been considering are shown in Table A.5.

TABLE 5.5   Sources: as for Figure 5.6.

TABLE 5.6   Sources: *National Income and Expenditure* for the relevant years.

TABLE 5.7   Sources: as for Table 5.6.

TABLE 5.8   Sources: as for Table 5.6.

TABLE 5.9   Sources: as for Table 5.6.

TABLE 5.10   Calculated from the four preceding tables.

TABLE 5.11   Sources: *National Income and Expenditure, Department of Employment Gazette.*

TABLE 5.12   Sources: as for Table 5.11.

TABLE 6.1   Sources: *Census of Population 1971, Economic Activity*, table 19, and *Census of Population 1961, Summary Tables*, table 31.

TABLE 6.2   Sources: as for Table 6.1.

TABLE 6.3   Sources: as for Table 6.1.

TABLE 6.4   Sources: as for Table 6.1.

TABLE 6.5   Sources: *Census of Population 1971, Economic Activity*, table 4, and *Census of Population 1961, Summary Tables*, table 31.

TABLE 6.6   Sources: *Census of Population 1971, Economic Activity*, table 16; *Census of Population 1961, Summary Tables*, table 36.

TABLE 6.7   Sources: *Census of Population 1971, Economic Activity*, table 16; *Department of Employment Gazette.*

TABLE A-5 'Real consumption' budget, 1954

		In 1974 terms (£)								
		9.81	15.40	23.36	26.40	32.14	39.85	54.59	75.35	128.43
£ 1974 individually reflated for each category	Food	3.68	6.29	10.28	10.49	12.14	13.01	17.76	19.84	23.61
	Durables	0.24	0.50	0.92	1.29	1.59	2.08	2.82	3.27	3.38
	Services	0.84	1.22	1.83	2.22	3.08	4.79	7.26	16.45	36.48
Above, as % of 'real consumption' budget	Food	37.5	40.8	44.0	39.7	37.8	32.6	32.5	26.3	18.4
	Durables	2.4	3.2	3.9	4.9	4.9	5.2	5.2	4.3	2.6
	Services	8.6	7.9	7.8	8.4	9.6	12.0	13.3	21.8	28.4

TABLE A.6 *Distribution of occupations across industries, 1971*

	Primary (agri-culture, mining)	Secondary (skilled, semi-skilled mfg.)	Intermediate (construc-tion, transport, unskilled labour)	Tertiary (admin., cleri-cal, sales)	Total (including unallocated)	Primary	Secondary	Intermediate	Tertiary
	% of workforce					*% of industry*			
1. Agriculture	2.465	0.039	0.080	0.134	2.724	90.5	1.4	2.9	4.9
2. Mines	0.986	0.270	0.206	0.216	1.680	58.7	16.1	12.3	12.9
3. Food	0.011	1.145	0.995	1.004	3.169	0.3	36.1	31.4	31.7
4. Coal products	–	0.090	0.062	0.100	0.253	–	35.6	24.5	39.5
5. Chemicals	0.007	0.746	0.409	0.890	1.968	0.4	37.9	20.8	45.2
6. Metal mfg.	0.002	1.136	0.658	0.561	2.363	0.1	48.1	27.8	23.7
7. Mech. eng.	0.004	2.602	0.635	1.571	4.828	0.1	53.9	13.1	32.5
8. Instrument eng.	–	0.339	0.060	0.223	0.623	–	54.4	9.6	35.8
9. Elec. eng.	0.003	1.943	0.403	1.255	3.612	0.1	53.8	11.2	34.7
10. Ships	–	0.477	0.154	0.141	0.774	–	61.6	19.9	18.2
11. Vehicles	0.002	1.969	0.510	0.892	3.385	0.1	58.2	15.1	26.4
12. Metal goods	0.001	1.519	0.395	0.589	2.514	–	60.4	15.7	23.4
13. Textiles	0.002	1.594	0.434	0.499	2.538	0.1	62.8	17.1	19.7
14. Leather	–	0.151	0.034	0.048	0.228	–	66.2	14.9	18.4
15. Clothes	0.001	1.494	0.127	0.390	2.017	–	74.1	6.3	19.3
16. Bricks	0.008	0.573	0.416	0.313	1.312	0.6	43.7	31.7	23.9
17. Timber	0.003	0.767	0.272	0.252	1.297	0.2	59.1	21.0	19.4
18. Paper	0.002	1.295	0.399	0.922	2.628	0.1	49.3	15.2	35.1
19. Other mfg.	0.001	0.775	0.250	0.361	1.394	0.1	55.6	17.9	25.9

TABLE A.6 (contd)

	Primary (agriculture, mining)	Secondary (skilled, semi-skilled mfg.)	Intermediate (construction, transport, unskilled labour)	Tertiary (admin., clerical, sales)	Total (including unallocated)	Primary	Secondary	Intermediate	Tertiary
			% of workforce				% of industry		
20. Construction	0.024	2.031	3.812	1.283	7.162	0.3	28.4	53.2	17.9
21. Utilities	0.004	0.508	0.361	0.678	1.555	0.3	32.7	23.2	43.6
22. Transport	0.003	0.874	3.943	1.870	6.711	–	13.0	58.8	27.9
23. Distribution	0.019	1.244	1.586	10.066	12.942	0.1	9.6	12.3	77.8
24. Finance	0.018	0.049	0.184	3.825	4.086	0.4	1.2	4.5	93.6
25. Professional	0.112	0.267	0.344	11.693	12.449	0.9	2.1	2.8	93.9
26. Misc. services	0.234	1.073	0.693	7.975	10.021	2.3	10.7	6.9	79.6
27. Administration	0.171	0.250	0.998	4.308	5.762	3.0	4.3	17.3	74.8

TABLE A.7 Distribution of occupations across industries, 1961

	Primary (agriculture, mining)	Secondary (skilled, semi-skilled mfg.)	Intermediate (construction, transport, unskilled labour)	Tertiary (admin., clerical, prof., sales)	Total (including unallocated)	Primary (agriculture, mining)	Secondary	Intermediate	Tertiary
			% of workforce					% of industry	
1. Agriculture	3.526	0.031	0.066	0.090	3.734	94.4	0.8	1.77	2.4
2. Mines	2.182	0.329	0.332	0.291	3.152	69.2	10.4	10.5	9.2
3. Food	0.007	1.004	1.097	0.912	3.072	0.2	32.7	35.7	29.7
4. Chemicals	0.006	0.726	0.532	0.884	2.176	0.3	33.3	24.4	40.6
5. Metals	0.002	1.346	0.801	0.554	2.734	—	49.2	29.3	20.3
6. Engineering	0.004	4.913	1.144	2.694	8.866	—	55.4	12.9	30.4
7. Ships	—	0.669	0.212	0.144	1.034	—	64.7	20.5	13.9
8. Vehicles	0.003	2.123	0.569	0.922	3.658	—	58.0	15.6	25.2
9. Metal goods n.e.s.	0.001	1.400	0.382	0.472	2.292	—	61.1	16.7	20.6
10. Textiles	0.003	2.369	0.492	0.535	3.450	—	68.7	14.3	15.5
11. Leather	—	0.180	0.032	0.047	0.264	—	68.2	12.1	17.8
12. Clothing	0.001	1.772	0.144	0.425	2.383	—	74.3	6.0	17.8
13. Bricks	0.009	0.640	0.463	0.270	1.403	0.6	45.6	33.0	19.2
14. Timber	0.007	0.796	0.285	0.223	1.330	0.5	59.8	21.4	16.8
15. Paper	0.002	1.419	0.408	0.781	2.643	—	53.7	15.4	29.5
16. Other mfg.	0.001	0.717	0.222	0.329	1.289	—	55.6	17.2	25.5

TABLE A.7 (contd)

	Primary (agriculture, mining)	Secondary (skilled, semi-skilled mfg.)	Intermediate (construction, transport, unskilled labour)	Tertiary (admin., clerical, prof., sales)	Total (including unallocated)	Primary	Secondary	Intermediate	Tertiary
	% of workforce					% of industry			
17. Construction	0.025	1.891	4.060	0.935	6.984	0.4	27.0	58.1	13.4
18. Utilities	0.004	0.560	0.488	0.576	1.648	0.2	34.0	29.6	35.0
19. Transport	0.003	0.832	4.745	1.646	7.304	–	11.4	65.0	22.5
20. Distribution	0.012	1.544	1.719	10.509	13.920	–	11.1	12.3	75.5
21. Finance	0.017	0.017	0.085	2.360	2.496	0.7	0.7	3.4	94.5
22. Professional	0.097	0.219	0.280	8.60	9.255	1.0	2.4	3.0	93.0
23. Misc. services	0.279	1.076	0.672	7.869	9.989	2.8	10.8	6.7	78.8
24. Administration	0.146	0.241	1.246	3.236	4.922	3.0	4.9	25.3	65.7

TABLE 6.8   Source: *Census of Population, 1971, Economic Activity*, table 19, 'Industry by Occupation'. Data is given in Table A.6.

TABLE 6.9   Sources: *Census of Population, 1961, England and Wales; Industry Tables*, table 7: *Scotland: Occupation, Industry and Workplace*, table 7. Data is given in Table A.7.

TABLE 6.10   Sources: as for Tables 6.8 and 6.9.

TABLE 6.11   Sources: as for Tables 6.8 and 6.9.

TABLE 6.12   Sources: as for Tables 6.8 and 6.9.

TABLE 6.13   Sources: *Census of Population 1961, Summary Tables*, table 31; *Census of Population 1971, Economic Activity*, table 13.

TABLE 6.14   Sources: as for Table 6.13.

TABLE 6.15   Sources: as for Table 6.13.

FIGURE 6.1   From Bacon and Eltis, *Britain's Economic Problem*, p. 13.

FIGURE 6.2   Sources: *British Labour Statistics 1886–1968, Department of Employment Gazette*. The categories used here are slightly different from those in Bacon and Eltis. They are precisely those formed as Minimum List Headings and Industrial Orders in the *Census of Employment*.

FIGURE 6.3   Sources: *Census of Population 1971; Department of Employment Gazette*, January 1972.

FIGURE 6.4   Source: Secretariat of the Economic Commission for Europe, *Economic Survey of Europe in 1969* (New York: United Nations, 1970) p. 88.

FIGURE 7.1   Source: *Department of Employment Gazette*.

FIGURE 7.2   Source: *Department of Employment Gazette*.

FIGURE 7.3   Sources: *British Labour Statistics 1886–1968*, table 149; *British Labour Statistics Yearbooks*, 1969–75; *Department of Employment Gazette*, July 1976. The complete table of values is given in Table A.8.

TABLE 7.1   Sources: as for Figure 7.2.

FIGURE 7.4   Source: as for Figure 7.3.

TABLE 7.2   Source: *Classification of Occupations 1970*, p. x.

TABLE 7.3   Source: *Classification of Occupations 1970*, appendix B.1

FIGURE 7.5   Sources: *Census of Population 1961, Industry Tables*, table 3: *Census of Population 1971, Economic Activity*, table 16.

FIGURE 7.6   Source: *British Labour Statistics 1886–1968*, tables 89, 90, 91, 205; *Economic Trends No 276*, p. 26.

FIGURE 7.7   Source: as for Figure 7.6. See Figure A.1.

FIGURE 7.8   Sources: *British Labour Statistics 1886–1968*, table 205; *Census of Production 1975*.
TABLE 8.1   Source: as for Table 6.8.

TABLE A.8   *Proportion of managerial and skilled workers in U.K. industry, 1964–75*

| % of workforce | All manufacturing industry | | Metal-using industry | |
	Managerial, etc.	Skilled manual	Managerial, etc.	Skilled manual
1964	23.8	33.0	27.2	30.0
1965	24.2	33.2	27.5	30.0
1966	25.0	32.9	28.2	29.1
1967	25.7	32.7	29.1	29.4
1968	26.2	31.9	28.9	29.6
1969			29.4	27.7
1970			30.3	27.5
1971			30.6	27.9
1972			31.3	27.9
1973			28.6	28.5
1974			28.5	28.0
1975			30.1	28.6

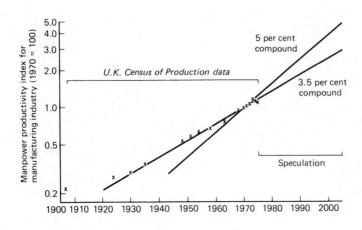

FIGURE A.1   *Manufacturing productivity growth in the United Kingdom, 1907–2005*

INDEX